You, Me, & Rest

CAROLINE HANNA GUIRGIS

WESTBOW
PRESS®
A DIVISION OF THOMAS NELSON
& ZONDERVAN

WestBow Press books may be ordered through booksellers or by contacting:

WestBow Press
A Division of Thomas Nelson & Zondervan
1663 Liberty Drive
Bloomington, IN 47403
www.westbowpress.com
844-714-3454

Scripture quotations are from The Holy Bible, English Standard Version® (ESV®), copyright © 2001 by Crossway, a publishing ministry of Good News Publishers. Used by permission. All rights reserved.

Scripture quotations are taken from the Holy Bible, New International Version®, NIV®. Copyright © 1973, 1978, 1984 by Biblica, Inc.™ Used by permission of Zondervan. All rights reserved worldwide.

ISBN: 979-8-3850-0359-4 (sc)
ISBN: 979-8-3850-0361-7 (hc)
ISBN: 979-8-3850-0360-0 (e)

Library of Congress Control Number: 2023913716

Print information available on the last page.

WestBow Press rev. date: 8/8/2023

CONTENTS

DEDICATION

To my two beautiful daughters, Danielle and Caitlyn,

This book is dedicated to both of you, my greatest blessings and sources of rest in the journey of motherhood. From the moment you entered my life, you brought peace and joy that transcends worldly understanding. Your growing faith, wisdom, and unconditional love have been a constant source of inspiration and comfort. In the chaos and demands of motherhood, you have been my guiding light, reminding me of the rest that can be found in the simple joys of everyday moments. Through your innocent eyes, I have witnessed the beauty of God's creation, and through your growing faith, I have discovered the transformative power of His love. Your unwavering support, understanding, and love have protected my weary soul. In moments of doubt, you have shown me the way forward, reminding me to trust in God's plan and to find rest in His embrace. Your compassion and empathy have reminded me of the importance of self-compassion and extending grace to myself as a mother. As you both continue to grow and navigate your journeys, I am in awe of the faith, wisdom, and strength you possess. Your unwavering belief in the goodness of God and your commitment to following His path inspire me daily. Through your examples, I have learned the true meaning of rest in the arms of our Heavenly Father. May this book serve as a testament to my immeasurable love and gratitude for both of you. As you read these pages, may you be reminded of the profound impact you have had on my life and the rest you have brought to my soul. May your faith continue to grow, and may your hearts always find solace in the rest that comes from knowing God's love. I thank God for giving you as my daughters, confidantes, and sources of rest. I am forever grateful for the gift of your presence in my life.

With all my love,
Your Mommy

PROLOGUE

THERE IS A longing deep within our souls for rest. It is a yearning to find comfort, peace, and relief from the burdens that weigh us down. This book is an invitation, a gentle call to step away from the noise and demands of life and enter that haven. Within these pages, you will discover a sanctuary where you can lay down your worries, hurts, and pain. It is a space where the weariness of your journey finds respite and where the wounds of your heart are tended to with care. In this journey, we will explore the depths of brokenness and the reality of pain, acknowledging the struggles that we face in our daily lives. Yet, woven throughout the narrative, there is a glimmer of hope, a promise that we can be rehabilitated and rejuvenated. It is an invitation to release the burdens we were never meant to carry alone and surrender them. As we embark on this voyage together, we will delve into timeless wisdom, drawing upon the stories of those who have walked the path of pain and found restoration. We will uncover the transformative power of faith, the beauty that can emerge from brokenness, and the purpose that can be discovered even in the darkest of seasons. Through reflective exercises, heartfelt reflections, and practical guidance, you will be encouraged to encompass vulnerability, seek healing, and open yourself up to rest. You are not alone in your struggles. Though we may not have traversed identical paths, it is evident that distinct struggles and challenges have marked our journeys. While the nature of these adversities may have diverged, the core emotions they evoke—pain, anguish, and heartache—remain universally understood. Despite the unique circumstances that shaped our experiences, we are united at the same level of hurt. This shared vulnerability, born from the empathy we foster for one another, bridges the gaps between our stories and allows us to connect on a profound and compassionate level. In recognizing and honoring the uniqueness of our struggles, we can forge a collective understanding that strengthens our bond and encourages a place of empathy, support, and healing.

In our pursuit of inner tranquility, we must confront the shadows of shame that linger from our past. Shame haunts us, weighing heavily on our hearts and minds and preventing us from living a healthy life. Breaking the cycle of shame ushers us into vulnerability, one of the most powerful tools in changing our world. People are seen and understood when we are transparent about our struggles and insecurities. It reinforces the understanding that we are not alone in our human experience. Because we all experience and process pain differently, coupled with the common struggle we face in regulating our emotions, it becomes all too easy to lose our way in the search for rest and peace. The unique methods we are wounded by can make identifying the specific remedies that will bring us solacement challenging. What may offer serenity to one person may not resonate with another. Furthermore, the difficulty in regulating our emotions can lead us down paths of turmoil, making it harder to find the rest we desperately need. It is essential to acknowledge and honor our individuality to regain our footing on the journey toward finding calm. Recognizing that our experiences and how we process emotions are unique allows us to explore various approaches and techniques that may bring us closer to harmony.

During my relentless pursuit of rest, I serendipitously encountered a fascinating concept that proved to be the pivotal catalyst propelling me into profound tranquility. As individuals, we have become accustomed to weathering the storms that life throws us. We summon our strength, resilience, and adaptability to navigate the chaos during these turbulent times. However, when the tempest subsides, and tranquility settles in, we often find ourselves at a loss for what to do next. The calmness feels unfamiliar, almost uncomfortable, as if we have grown so accustomed to battling against the winds that we have forgotten how to bask in the serenity. Consequently, without turmoil, we unintentionally create our storms. Restlessness creeps in, and we seek out chaos to fill our void. We do not inherently crave conflict or upheaval; our innate need for challenge and purpose propels us to stir calm.

Being calm in the storm and then a storm in the calm, I experienced the profound paradox of intrusive strength and its repercussions. It is a thought-provoking concept that encapsulates my ability to maintain composure and serenity during tumultuous situations while also possessing the power to incite unrest when everything seems tranquil. Talking about being calm in the storm signifies my capacity to find inner peace and stability amidst adversity. It is about cultivating resilience and emotional balance in the face of chaos, allowing me to think, make rational decisions, and navigate through turbulence gracefully. This state of calmness enables me to remain centered, composed, and adaptable, even when external circumstances are overwhelming. By embracing this mindset, I become less susceptible to chaos and can respond to challenges with greater control and clarity. However, there are times when I become a storm in the calm. This means my strength, dormant during quiet periods, suddenly awakens and disrupts the tranquility. It expresses my intensity, drive, and desire for change that stillness cannot contain. This unrest within compels me to challenge the status quo, initiate innovation, and inspire others to act. It is a force that stirs calm. While being a storm in the calm can be empowering, it also comes with consequences. The unrest causes discomfort and resistance as I push boundaries. Being a storm in the calm negatively affected me, leading to distress. The oxymoron that once held intrigue now reveals its detrimental consequences on my well-being. Becoming a storm in the calm brought me unintended turmoil and unrest, disrupting the stillness I longed for. The constant need to challenge the status quo and initiate change became overwhelming and a heavy burden on me. In hindsight, I now realize the importance of finding an equilibrium between calmness and a storm in the calm. It requires self-reflection, emotional intelligence, and responsiveness.

By recognizing this tendency, we can learn to find balance in both the stormy and peaceful moments of life, embracing stillness when it comes and using it as an opportunity for self-reflection, growth, and recharging our spirits. Remembering that rest is necessary and requires carving out moments of stillness and quiet amidst the noise of everyday life. It allows you to pause, breathe, and recharge your weary mind, body, and soul. It is the foundation upon which resilience, creativity, and growth thrive. It might be found in the solitude of nature, the warmth of an enjoyable book, or the laughter shared with loved ones. It could be a quiet meditation, a rejuvenating hobby, or simply allowing yourself to unplug and embrace the silence. Prioritize your well-being and make self-care a non-negotiable part of your routine. Embrace the ebb and flow of life, and find solace in the moments of rest, for they will nourish your soul and empower you to face the world with renewed strength. You deserve rest, my dear reader. Embrace, cherish, and let it guide your journey toward a life of balance, joy, and fulfillment.

CHAPTER 1

Broken Crayons
Still Color

CONVENIENTLY NESTLED JUST across the street from my apartment building in Staten Island, New York, stood the elementary school that would set my first day in kindergarten. Yet, despite its proximity, stepping into the halls of that unfamiliar environment marked a momentous occasion for me. I was the pioneer in my family, the first to embark on the American schooling experience. My parents had bravely journeyed from Egypt in 1970, seeking new opportunities and a better future for our family. Thus, with their dreams and aspirations intertwined with my own, I carried the weight of this significant milestone on my small shoulders. Against this backdrop, my teacher apprised our class of an upcoming fire drill to be conducted later in the week. English was not yet firmly rooted in my linguistic repertoire, as Arabic served as my primary language, so the concept of a fire drill remained elusive. Consequently, when recounting the day's events to my parents, I inadvertently conveyed that a fire would occur at school. Naturally skeptical, my father promptly reached out to the school to gain clarity on the matter. Subsequently, the principal assuaged his concerns and elucidated the necessity and importance of a fire drill. Patiently, my father relayed the routine and diligently rehearsed it with me at home. The scheduled training was set to take place toward the end of the week, and every evening leading up to that momentous day, we dedicated ourselves to its practice.

I felt adequately prepared on the morning of the drill, although the precise timing remained uncertain. Yet that uncertainty was intrinsic to the nature of the training. Seated around a circular table with a few fellow students, we occupied ourselves with coloring activities. Throughout the morning, we exclusively employed a single crayon, its fluorescent pink hue captivating our attention. Alas, as fate would have it, the crayon snapped, yet we persevered in our artistic endeavors, utilizing the fragmented remnants of our favored coloring tool. Just as it was my turn to resume coloring, the fire alarm unexpectedly blared to life, its shrill resonance jolting me. However, my mind was preoccupied more with the broken crayon than the commotion around me. Instead of obediently aligning myself with the teacher's instructions and joining the line of students, I remained seated at my desk, covertly concealing the crayon within the recesses of my mouth to ensure its preservation. In silence, we evacuated the classroom, with the teacher complying with my father's plea, keeping me nearby. We stood outside silently for several minutes, during which the teacher repeatedly inquired about my sense of safety. I could only nod, for my mouth was preoccupied with safeguarding the broken crayon, rendering me unable to speak.

Upon returning to the classroom and resuming our seats, I retrieved the crayon from my mouth, drying it off discreetly. The teacher, however, caught sight of this act and approached me with a gentle yet inquisitive demeanor. "Caroline, was that a crayon in your mouth?" Reluctantly, I nodded in affirmation. She probed further, "Why did you do that?" I explained that it was my favorite color and, as it had finally become my turn, I wished to seize the opportunity to color with it. In response, she offered a warm smile and embraced me tenderly. She retrieved a new crayon, identical in color, from the supply cabinet and requested that I surrender the broken crayon in exchange for a new replacement. However, I clutched the fractured remains with unwavering determination, unwilling to part with it. Looking into her eyes, I uttered, "Broken crayons still color." A moment of contemplation ensued before she replied, "You are correct, Caroline ... even broken crayons possess the capacity to create beautiful colors." Consequently, I was permitted to retain my cherished broken crayon. This episode merely represents a fraction of the overarching narrative within this chapter. The essence of this book lies not solely in my initial encounter with a fire drill but rather in the profound connection between you, the reader, and me. Together, we shall embark on a transformative journey through life, sharing triumphs and tribulations, moments of fracture, and subsequent healing.

Crayons, emblematic of our existence, are not the sole entities prone to breakage. We succumb to the hardships that befall us on life's unpredictable path. No individual can entirely evade the clutches of adversity. My response to this reality extends beyond mere sympathy, encompassing profound empathy. Empathy, as defined by the *Minds Journal*, represents the capacity to immerse oneself in another person's emotional landscape and perspective, harnessing this understanding to guide our actions. Hence, I deeply comprehend the immense anguish you may be experiencing. While my awareness of your pain may not alleviate its intensity, this book endeavors to accompany you through the labyrinth of suffering, illuminating the path with hope. During my most arduous trials, I truly grasped the meaning of hope. At moments when I believed I had reached the precipice of my existence, with nowhere else to turn, I inadvertently discovered new avenues to traverse. Growing up, religion was not merely a choice; it constituted the very fabric of my being. Growing up in a devout household gave me invaluable tools and knowledge but did not shield me from life's afflictions. I cannot deny the efficacy of discipline and intellectual pursuits. Nonetheless, a chasm persisted. For years, I struggled to bridge that divide.

In my initial publication, *The Beginning Starts at the End*, I bared my soul, candidly recounting my trials and losses. Despite my adversities, I triumphed with resilience and victory, not through my fortitude but by tapping into an even greater power within me. However, this story did not culminate with the publication of my first book; it marked but the commencement of a new chapter yet to unfold. The question "What's next?" reverberated within me, evoking profound emotions. There existed a purpose behind the trials I confronted, lessons to be learned and imparted. Given our innate need for connection and community, the lessons we glean from life are meant to be shared, enabling others to grow and evolve. Like the radiant broken crayon of fluorescent pink, I aspired to infuse vibrancy and color into the lives of those around me. Genuine hope possesses the remarkable ability to reassemble our shattered pieces, forging a renewed version of ourselves. If you yearn for such hope, I implore you to keep reading and unearth the joy that awaits you. In pursuing what seemed elusive, I found myself relentlessly pursued by that which I sought. Yet, in the sweet surrender, the moment of release, I discovered the profound gift of ultimate rest. I chased after dreams, desires, and aspirations, driven by a yearning that seemed insatiable. Yet the more I ran, the further they seemed to slip from my grasp. It was as if the essence of what I longed for pursued me, whispering in the wind, beckoning me to stop and let go. And so, in a moment of surrender, I ceased my striving. I relinquished the need to control, to force outcomes, and surrendered to the current of life's unfolding. In that surrender, I found a peace that surpassed understanding, a respite from the wild chase. Rest became my sanctuary, not merely in the physical sense but in the depths of my being. It was a place where the world's demands, expectations, and illusions lost their grip. It was a space where my soul could breathe, where the noise of the external world was muted, and the whispers of my heart grew louder. In that surrender, I discovered a freedom that transcended circumstances.

I realized that true rest does not depend on external circumstances aligning perfectly but resides in the state of our hearts. It is an inner sanctuary we carry within, a haven of peace that remains undisturbed amid the ebb and flow of life. In the ultimate surrender, I found rest in acceptance, embracing the present moment as it unfolded. I learned to let go of the burdensome weight of expectations and found peace in the beauty of what is. It was a gentle reminder that true fulfillment lies not in the pursuit of what we do not yet possess but in the profound appreciation of the gifts we have been given. Let us acknowledge that in the surrender lies the path to ultimate rest. When we release our grip and relinquish the need to control and strive, we open ourselves to the vastness of possibility. There, we discover the transformative power of rest, the serenity that envelops our souls, and the boundless joy accompanying our journey through life. Selah!

At the end of each chapter, you will see the word *selah*. *Selah* is found frequently in the book of Psalms in the Bible, particularly in the Hebrew Psalter. While its exact meaning remains uncertain, scholars and translators offer various interpretations. Some proposed purposes include:

1. Pause or rest: One interpretation suggests that *selah* serves as a musical notation, indicating a pause or rest in the music. It could be a moment for reflection, allowing the reader or musician to pause and contemplate the words or themes expressed in the preceding verses.

2. Lift or exalt: Another perspective suggests that *selah* could mean to lift or exalt. It may prompt the reader to raise their voice in praise, lifting their thoughts and emotions to a higher spiritual plane.

3. *Amen* or *so be it*: Some scholars propose that *selah* is akin to the word *amen* and signifies affirmation or agreement with the content of the preceding text. It could serve as a call to acknowledge and embrace the terms' truth or as a response to the agreement, reinforcing the message.

4. Change or transition: Another interpretation is that *selah* indicates a change or growth in the structure or flow of the psalm. It could mark a shift in tone, theme, or musical arrangement, highlighting a new section or emphasizing a significant point.

After each chapter's revelations, surrender your mind to the tranquil embrace of stillness, for it is in these sacred moments that true wholeness awaits. As you grant yourself the gift of rest, a special connection with the Ultimate Healer unfolds. In the serenity of silence and solitude, breathe slowly, for with every inhale and exhale, you draw closer to the Divine. This intimate encounter is yours alone, a personal journey that resonates deeply within your soul. Behold the power of being still and knowing that there is a God. Regardless of belief, every breath you take reminds you of His existence. He is the essence of life, the source of every heartbeat. So, I implore you to sit and surrender, allowing His presence to envelop you completely. You will perceive this sacred stillness with the clarity of heart, mind, and soul. Like an eagle soaring on the currents of faith, you will be lifted to new heights of understanding. Your spirit will be renewed, and your being restored to its inherent wholeness.

I have fervently prayed for you, dear reader, and my faith in your transformation is unwavering. I believe in the miracles that await you as you embrace this journey toward wholeness. May your soul be refreshed, your heart awakened, and your mind enlightened as you bask in the restorative power of stillness. Embrace the divine connection that emerges in these moments of respite, for it is there that you will find the answers you seek and the strength to overcome. So, rest, believe, and soar on the wings of wholeness. Your restoration is at hand, and a glorious new chapter awaits.

THIS IS YOUR PERSONAL SPACE

WRITE HOW YOU WILL

REFRESH, ESCAPE, SOOTHE, TRANQUILIZE

Let. Yourself -REST-

DATE:

I WILL REST TODAY BY...

CHAPTER 2

Triumph over Stigma

TO UNEARTH THE hidden reservoirs of joy that lie dormant within our souls, we must first cast off the shackles of shame, that insidious force known as Self-Hatred and Misunderstood Emotions. Lysa Terkhurst astutely encapsulates its essence as Self-Hatred at My Expense, a complex emotional tapestry woven from perceived failures, profound inadequacy, and an overwhelming sense of unworthiness. Shame, a formidable and distressing presence, wields the power to isolate, erode self-confidence, and diminish our inherent value. It is an emotion that touches us all, irrespective of our station in life, yet it is imperative to remember that shame does not define our essence or intrinsic worth. To conquer this formidable foe, we must first acknowledge its existence and bravely confront the triggers and deeply ingrained beliefs perpetuating its grip upon our spirits. Indeed, shame represents the culmination of self-hatred, the insidious whispers of negative self-talk and evil thoughts that corrode our very beings, hardening our hearts and rendering us prone to frequent and abrupt fractures. The aftermath of such fractures manifests as an inability to trust, express emotions authentically, or forge profound connections with others. In its merciless grip, shame closes our eyes to the abundant joys that beckon, obscuring the essence of happiness. While the experience of shame is multifaceted and often convoluted, it can also catalyze positive change, motivating us to transcend our past behaviors and embrace growth.

The arduous path to overcoming shame begins with a fundamental shift in our internal dialogue, challenging the distorted, pessimistic, self-critical, and self-defeating thoughts that perpetuate its hold. External stressors, anxiety, depression, or the indelible imprints of past experiences often trigger these destructive thoughts. Confronting shame requires a profound shift in our mindset, a courageous confrontation with our past mistakes and missteps, rather than seeking solace in denial. The corrosive power of pride must be acknowledged and overcome, for it only nourishes and exacerbates our shame. In this transformative journey, we must not seek absolution through evasion but endeavor to heal our hearts through introspection and forgiveness. Confronting shame is a testament to our commitment to growth and the reconciliation of our hearts, paving the way for self-forgiveness and the capacity to extend forgiveness to others. This challenging undertaking demands that we forsake the crutch of excuses, standing boldly against the onslaught of shame's grip and vanquishing it with unwavering resolve. Should the need arise, we should never hesitate to seek support from loved ones, trusted friends, or mental health professionals who can provide guidance and compassion. The transformative power of sharing our experiences and emotions cannot be underestimated, for it offers us a broader perspective, infuses us with newfound strength, and equips us with more effective coping strategies.

Now, let us collectively incorporate the audacious challenge of unburdening ourselves from the oppressive weight of shame. Let us proceed with unwavering courage, fortifying our spirits against the relentless assault of self-doubt and stepping into the vibrancy of a life liberated from shame's suffocating grasp. In this defining moment of self-discovery and transformation, we collectively confront the formidable task of shedding the suffocating cloak of shame that has burdened our hearts for far too long. We embark upon a profound introspection and self-empowerment journey, arming ourselves against the relentless onslaught of self-doubt that has stifled our growth and impeded our joy. We no longer succumb to its whispers of self-hatred and unworthiness. Instead, we rise above the paralyzing grip of shame, fortifying our hearts with a resolute determination to reclaim our inherent value and embrace the full spectrum of our authentic selves. With each step we take, we chip away at the foundations of shame's stronghold, dismantling the distorted beliefs and negative self-perceptions that have held us captive. We challenge our past mistakes or perceived inadequacies to define our worth. In this daring act of self-liberation, we recognize that our worth transcends our flaws and encompasses the limitless potential for growth, resilience, and transformation. As we navigate this uncharted territory, we find solace in the unwavering support of our loved ones and form a steadfast community bound by empathy, compassion, and the shared determination to emerge from the shadow of shame and into the radiant light of self-acceptance. Through vulnerability and open-hearted connection, we offer one another a safe space to express our deepest fears, insecurities, and pain. In this sacred exchange, we discover the healing balm of understanding and shared experiences, strengthening our resolve to face shame head-on and emerge victoriously. As we forge ahead, our lives transform into a vibrant tableau with authenticity, resilience, and self-love. Liberated from the suffocating grasp of shame, we embrace our unique narratives with unabashed pride, celebrating the journey that has shaped us into the remarkable individuals we are today. No longer defined by our past transgressions or the limitations imposed by shame, we step into the realm of possibility, guided by a newfound sense of purpose and self-compassion. In this shared endeavor, we discover the transformative power of forgiveness — both for ourselves and others. We recognize that the path to liberation requires us to release the weight of resentment and self-condemnation, replacing it with the gentle embrace of forgiveness and understanding. As we extend forgiveness to ourselves, we acknowledge that our mistakes do not define us but serve as catalysts for growth and wisdom. In turn, we offer forgiveness to those who may have contributed to our feelings of shame, recognizing their fallibility and the transformative potential of compassion.

For those seeking guidance in navigating the intricate process of overcoming shame, an invaluable resource worth exploring is "The Soul of Shame: Retelling the Stories, We Believe About Ourselves." Indulge in the enlightening realm of "The Soul of Shame: A Profound Exploration of the Constraining Power of Shame within the Human Psyche," penned by the esteemed psychiatrist and erudite scholar Dr. Kurt Thompson. Prepare to embark on an intellectual odyssey as Thompson deftly navigates the intricate dimensions of shame, drawing upon a rich connection of psychological, neurological, and spiritual perspectives to illuminate its profound impact on our personal and interpersonal spheres. With eloquence, Thompson posits that shame, an indomitable emotional experience, wields a pervasive influence on our self-perception, interrelationships, and overall holistic well-being. Peering through the lens of meticulous examination, he unveils the intricate neural circuitry through which shame configures our cognitive processes, behavioral repertoire, and emotional landscape, laying bare the neurobiological underpinnings that imprison us. Moreover, he astutely dissects the formative origins of shame, often enshrined within the crucible of our formative years, and its surreptitious integration into the very fabric of our self-identity. At the heart of Thompson's treatise lies a compelling call to reassess and reconceptualize the narratives and paradigms that shape our self-conception. Through a metacognitive journey into the recesses of our innermost stories, he boldly asserts that we possess the potential to challenge and transcend the oppressive grasp of shame. In this transformative endeavor, Thompson extols the virtues of empathy, compassion, and vulnerability as catalysts for personal healing, nurturing the growth of wholesome relationships that flourish within and without. "The Soul of Shame" delves even further, seamlessly intertwining a spiritual dimension that beckons us to contemplate shame through the prism of the Christian faith. Here, Thompson skillfully weaves theological insights, illuminating a redemptive framework that serves as a guiding light for navigating the labyrinthine depths of shame, bestowing solace and renewal upon those who seek a spiritually informed path to healing. In summation, "The Soul of Shame" stands as an erudite magnum opus, an intricately composed symphony of intellectual inquiry that orchestrates a harmonious fusion of psychological, neurological, and spiritual perspectives. It beckons the curious minds and the longing souls, inviting them to embark upon an illuminating quest where liberation from shame becomes an attainable reality, and the reclamation of our inherent dignity becomes an indelible triumph.

The power of reading books like the one above is immeasurable, transcending mere language and extending its influence into our thoughts, emotions, and actions. Words can shape our perception of ourselves, others, and the world. When we use positive comments, we uplift and inspire ourselves and those who hear or read them. Affirmative words have the potential to ignite hope, boost self-confidence, and foster resilience in times of adversity. They can heal wounds, mend broken spirits, and bridge divides. Whether spoken or written, constructive words have a ripple effect, spreading joy, encouragement, and optimism to all who encounter them. They can transform attitudes, shift perspectives, and create a nurturing and supportive environment. Let us never underestimate the profound impact of words and the transformative potential they hold within our lives and the lives of others. Within the pages of the Bible, I discovered an extraordinary wellspring of power emanating from the words that grace its sacred text. Each verse and passage carry a timeless wisdom that resonates deep within my soul, providing guidance and strength. The words I read in the Bible possess an unparalleled ability to ignite faith, instill hope, and inspire profound transformation. They constantly remind us of the divine love, grace, and purpose encompassing our existence. Through the stories, teachings, and promises embedded within its verses, the Bible offers a beacon of light amidst the darkness, a balm for the weary spirit, and a source of unwavering reassurance. It is within these words that I am freed from shame. The power derived from the terms of the Bible is both transcendent and transformative, shaping my beliefs, character, and actions and instilling in me an unwavering sense of purpose and divine connection.

Using scripture to overcome shame holds immense value for individuals seeking healing, restoration, and liberation from the burdens of self-condemnation. Scripture provides a divine perspective on our worth and identity. It reminds us that we are created in the image of God and deeply loved by Him. By anchoring ourselves in the truth of God's Word, we can combat the lies and distorted self-perceptions that shame often imposes upon us. It reminds us that through Christ, we have been redeemed and set free from the chains of guilt and condemnation. Scripture reassures us that there is always an opportunity for renewal and transformation regardless of our past mistakes or shortcomings. Many passages in the Bible offer promises of restoration, healing, and a future filled with hope. They remind us that, despite our experiences of shame, God can turn our brokenness into wholeness and grant us a new beginning. These promises instill a sense of optimism and encourage us to press forward with courage and perseverance. Scripture provides encouragement, strength, and comfort in times of shame and distress. It offers stories of individuals who have faced similar struggles and found redemption, reminding us that we are not alone in our journey. These accounts allow us to draw inspiration and find the strength to overcome shame. Engaging with scripture will enable us to invite the transformative power of the Holy Spirit into our lives. The Word of God can penetrate deep within our hearts, renewing our minds and reshaping our perspectives. It enables us to understand our inherent worth better and live in alignment with God's truth. Scripture can be a unifying force within a community of believers. When approached with an open heart and a willingness to seek truth and transformation, scripture can be a powerful tool in overcoming shame.

In the ancient city of Jericho, a woman named Rahab was entangled in a web of shame and societal condemnation. She was known as a harlot, a label that burdened her with the weight of judgment and scorn. Yet, within Rahab's heart, a spark of resilience and a yearning for redemption burned. As the Israelites, led by Joshua, approached Jericho, Rahab's life took an unexpected turn. Hearing tales of the Israelite's mighty God and the miracles they had witnessed, Rahab's spirit stirred with newfound hope. She saw an opportunity for salvation, not only for herself but for her family as well. Risking her own life, Rahab chose to harbor two Israelite spies who had come to scout the city. In an act of courage and faith, she hid them on her rooftop, covering their presence from the authorities. Rahab confessed her belief in the God of the Israelites and pleaded for mercy and protection. In return for her kindness and faith, the spies solemnly promised Rahab. They assured her that when the Israelites conquered Jericho, her life and the lives of her loved ones would be spared. They instructed her to hang a scarlet cord from her window as a sign for the Israelite forces to recognize her dwelling and keep her safe. When the walls of Jericho eventually fell, the Israelites captured the city. True to their word, Rahab and her family were saved while the rest of Jericho faced destruction. Rahab's act of bravery and her unwavering trust in God had not only shielded her from shame but also positioned her as a pivotal figure in the lineage of Jesus Christ. Rahab's story is a powerful testament to the transformative power of grace and redemption. Her past as a harlot did not define her future. Through her bold actions and faith, she overcame the chains of shame, finding her place in the lineage of Jesus Himself. Rahab's legacy reminds us that we can rise above our circumstances no matter our past or the labels society may impose upon us. We can reshape our destinies and contribute to a greater purpose through courage, faith, and unwavering trust in a higher power. Rahab's journey from shame to significance is an eternal reminder that redemption knows no bounds and that our past does not have to dictate our future.

Are you seeking refuge from shame? God's love knows no boundaries and extends far beyond the confines of any faith or belief system. It is a love that embraces all of humanity, transcending religious labels and divisions. With open arms, God invites every person, regardless of their background, culture, or religious affiliation, to experience His boundless grace and mercy. His divine invitation reaches out to all, beckoning us to seek Him, to know Him, and to find relief in His unconditional love. God's inclusivity is a testament to His infinite compassion and understanding, affirming that His love is not limited to a select few but extends to all willing to open their hearts and receive it. In this sincere invitation, we discover the beauty of a God who encompasses and cherishes every soul, embracing the diversity of humanity and drawing us closer to the unity that transcends all barriers. The following scriptures from the Bible offer reassurance and encouragement to anyone seeking to overcome shame. They remind us of God's love, forgiveness, and the transformative power of faith, providing a firm foundation for healing and restoration.

Selah

Take a moment to reflect on the profound meaning within the verses below. Engage in this reflective exercise as a personal conversation between you and the Divine. Prayer, esteemed as a living word, resonates as a profound and dynamic expression of spirituality. It embodies the essence of a deep connection between humanity and the divine, transcending mere recitation or ritualistic practice. In prayer, words acquire an inherent vitality infused with intention, faith, and a profound yearning for communion. As a living word, prayer breathes life into the depths of our being, fostering a sacred dialogue that transcends the limitations of language. It becomes a vehicle through which we articulate our innermost thoughts, desires, and vulnerabilities to a higher power, inviting divine presence to illuminate our path. Through prayer, we encounter the transformative power of the sacred, experiencing peace, guidance, and profound moments of connection that transcend the boundaries of the physical realm. Moreover, prayer reverberates beyond the individual domain, resonating within the communal fabric of faith. It invites us to explore the depths of our spiritual existence, seeks meaning and purpose, and cultivates a sense of awe and reverence for the mysteries surrounding us. As we pray, we participate in a sacred dance where our words intertwine with the divine, breathing life into our spirits and illuminating our faith journey.

1. Romans 8:1-2 - "Therefore, there is no condemnation for those in Christ Jesus, because through Christ Jesus the law of the Spirit who gives life has set you free from the law of sin and death."

2. Psalm 34:4 - "I sought the Lord, and he answered me; he delivered me from all my fears."

3. Isaiah 61:7 - "Instead of your shame you will receive a double portion, and instead of disgrace you will rejoice in your

inheritance. And so, you will inherit a double portion in your land, and everlasting joy will be yours."

4. 1 Peter 2:6 - "For in Scripture it says: 'See, I lay a stone in Zion, a chosen and precious cornerstone, and the one who trusts in him will never be put to shame.'"

5. Isaiah 54:4 - "Do not be afraid; you will not be put to shame. Do not fear disgrace; you will not be humiliated. You will forget the shame of your youth and remember no more the reproach of your widowhood."

6. Hebrews 12:2 - "Fixing our eyes on Jesus, the pioneer, and perfecter of faith. For the joy set before him, he endured the cross, scorning its shame, and sat down at the right hand of the throne of God."

7. Psalm 25:3 - "No one who hopes in you will ever be put to shame, but shame will come on those who are treacherous without cause."

8. 2 Corinthians 5:17 - "Therefore, if anyone is in Christ, the new creation has come: The old has gone, the new is here!"

9. Joel 2:25 - "I will repay you for the years the locusts have eaten—the great locust and the young locust, the other locusts, and the locust swarm—my great army that I sent among you."

10. Romans 10:11 - "As Scripture says, 'Anyone who believes in him will never be put to shame.'"

THIS IS YOUR PERSONAL SPACE

WRITE HOW YOU WILL

REFRESH, ESCAPE, SOOTHE, TRANQUILIZE

Let. yourself -REST-

DATE:

I WILL REST TODAY BY...

CHAPTER 3

Discovering Wholeness
Beyond Shame

AFTER TRIUMPHANTLY OVERCOMING the stifling grip of shame, a new horizon dawns, beckoning us toward the transformative depths of wholeness. As we shed the burdensome weight of self-condemnation and embrace our inherent worth, a profound journey of healing and restoration unfolds. This fundamental chapter delves into the deep truths that pave the way to lasting joy and a sense of home, even amidst our brokenness. We explore the remarkable power of vulnerability as a gateway to connection and authenticity. By shedding the protective layers that shield us from shame, we open ourselves up to meaningful relationships and cultivate a sense of belonging that transcends our brokenness. Together, we navigate the delicate dance of vulnerability, empowering ourselves and others to forge deep connections that nurture our souls. In humanity, vulnerability emerges as a beacon of profound strength and harmony. As we traverse the path of wholeness, we uncover the remarkable power inherent in embracing vulnerability. This section delves into the transformative nature of exposure, illuminating its ability to nurture authentic connections, cultivate empathy, and unlock the door to profound joy and belonging. At its core, vulnerability is the courageous act of allowing ourselves to be seen, stripped of the masks and facades that shield us from the world. It is a radical departure from the armor of shame, inviting others to witness our true selves—flawed, imperfect, and beautifully human. As we shed the shackles of fear and embrace vulnerability, we discover that our authenticity becomes the fertile ground upon which genuine connections are formed.

Vulnerability acts as a catalyst for cultivating empathy, the capacity to understand and share in the experiences of others. As we open ourselves, we foster an environment where compassion flourishes, breaking down the barriers that separate us. In our shared vulnerability, we recognize the universal nature of the human struggle, and a profound sense of empathy arises, forging deep connections that transcend the boundaries of shame and isolation. It allows us to understand our imperfections and celebrate the beauty of our unique journeys. Rather than striving for an unattainable ideal of perfection, we recognize that our brokenness holds the seeds of authenticity and growth. Through vulnerability, we permit ourselves to let go of the need for a model, and in doing so, we free ourselves - the imperfect yet infinitely valuable beings that we are. It becomes the cornerstone upon which trust and intimacy are built. We create a sacred space where faith can thrive by daring to reveal our deepest truths, fears, and aspirations. We invite others to do the same in opening ourselves up to vulnerability. It becomes the key that unlocks the door to profound joy and liberation.

In the biblical narrative, King David emerges as a complex figure, displaying remarkable vulnerability amidst his triumphs and challenges. Despite his status as a powerful and revered king, David's life was far from immune to the struggles and vulnerabilities inherent to human experience. One poignant example of David's vulnerability can be found in the Psalms, where he bears his soul before God. David pours out his deepest emotions through the poetic verses, laying bare his fears, doubts, joys, and sorrows. In these intimate prayers and songs, we witness a man unafraid to confront his weaknesses and shortcomings, seeking guidance from a higher power. David's vulnerability is exemplified in his moments of repentance. When faced with his grave transgressions, such as his affair with Bathsheba and the subsequent murder of her husband Uriah, David displays genuine remorse. He acknowledges his sins, confesses them openly, and seeks forgiveness with a contrite heart. In doing so, David reveals his humility and willingness to face the consequences of his actions, highlighting a vulnerability in the face of his moral failings. David's vulnerability can be seen in his relationships with others. He connects deeply with individuals such as Jonathan, whose friendship and loyalty deeply touched his heart. David's lamentation over Jonathan's death in 2 Samuel 1 highlights his raw emotions and vulnerability in mourning the loss of a dear companion. David's journey serves as a reminder that vulnerability is not a sign of weakness but a testament to one's authenticity and willingness to confront the depths of their humanity. David's example encourages us to cultivate openness and honesty in our lives, acknowledging our vulnerabilities and seeking support and guidance from a loving and compassionate source.

Vulnerability, often associated with strength and authenticity, is crucial in effective leadership. Contrary to the traditional notion of leaders as stoic and invulnerable, embracing vulnerability allows leaders to forge genuine connections, build trust, and foster a more inclusive and supportive environment. Leaders who demonstrate vulnerability create a space where team members feel safe to express themselves openly and honestly. By sharing their challenges, doubts, and mistakes, leaders encourage others to do the same, fostering an atmosphere of trust and psychological safety. When team members see their leader being vulnerable, it humanizes them, making them relatable and approachable. This, in turn, encourages collaboration, innovation, and the sharing of diverse perspectives, leading to stronger decision-making and problem-solving. Furthermore, vulnerability in leadership cultivates empathy and understanding. By openly acknowledging their stations, leaders demonstrate humility and a willingness to learn from others. This fosters a culture of kindness, where team members feel valued and heard, knowing their leader is receptive to their experiences and perspectives. Such an environment promotes cooperation, creativity, and a sense of belonging, enabling individuals to bring their whole selves to the table and contribute their best work. In addition, vulnerability enhances resilience and adaptability within teams. Leaders who acknowledge uncertainties and share their exposure during challenging times empower their team to confront adversity with courage and grace. By openly addressing setbacks and failures, leaders inspire resilience, demonstrating that lapses are not indicative of individual inadequacies but opportunities for growth and learning. Importantly, vulnerability in leadership is not synonymous with weakness or ineffectiveness. Rather, it highlights a leader's authenticity, humility, and willingness to be transparent. It takes courage to be vulnerable, requiring stepping outside the comfort zone and embracing the inherent risks. However, the rewards are substantial - enhanced team dynamics, increased employee engagement, and a culture of trust and collaboration. Leaders who embrace vulnerability create environments that promote growth, foster resilience, and nurture the full potential of their teams. Leading authentically and humbly inspires and empowers others to reach their highest potential, forging a path toward collective success.

The depth of vulnerability's impact on the intricate workings of our brain beckons us to embark on a soul-stirring self-exploration. It serves as an invitation to plunge into the depths of our being, unearthing the raw authenticity that resides within. This profound understanding compels us to embrace vulnerability as an integral part of our human experience, allowing its transformative power to guide us toward a more genuine existence. By heeding this call, we embark on a sacred journey towards self-discovery, unearthing the treasures hidden within and illuminating the path to profound personal growth and connection. Vulnerability can profoundly affect the brain, influencing various cognitive and emotional processes. When we allow ourselves to be vulnerable, several key changes occur in the brain:

1. Increased activation in the emotional centers: Vulnerability often elicits strong emotions such as fear, anxiety, or openness. These emotions activate brain regions, such as the amygdala, responsible for processing and generating emotional responses. The heightened activation in these areas can lead to a deeper emotional experience and a greater awareness of our internal state.

2. Enhanced social connection and empathy: Vulnerability can foster deeper relationships with others. Research suggests that expressing vulnerability activates brain regions associated with social bonding and heart, such as the anterior cingulate

cortex and the insula. These regions help us understand and relate to the emotions of others, facilitating stronger interpersonal connections.

3. Increased cognitive flexibility and learning: Opening us to vulnerability can promote cognitive flexibility and understanding. By stepping outside our comfort zones and embracing uncertainty, we engage brain regions associated with adaptation and growth, such as the prefrontal cortex and the hippocampus. These regions involve decision-making, problem-solving, and memory formation, allowing us to navigate new or challenging situations better.

4. Reduced stress response: Vulnerability can help reduce stress and anxiety. Sharing our vulnerabilities with trusted individuals activates brain regions associated with social support and emotional regulation, such as the prefrontal and ventromedial prefrontal cortex. These regions can modulate the stress response and promote calm and emotional stability.

5. Increased self-awareness and introspection: Vulnerability encourages self-reflection and meditation, which can activate brain regions associated with self-awareness, such as the medial prefrontal cortex. This increased self-awareness allows us to gain insight into our emotions, thoughts, and motivations, leading to personal growth and self-discovery.

Overall, vulnerability has a multifaceted impact on the brain, influencing emotional processing, social connection, cognitive flexibility, stress regulation, and self-awareness. By understanding these effects, we can appreciate the transformative power of vulnerability and its potential to facilitate personal growth, resilience, and deeper human connections.

The vulnerability of C.S. Lewis, the esteemed author, and scholar, unveils a profound dimension of his literary and personal journey. Beneath the eloquent prose and intellectual prowess lies a tender openness and an unguarded heart that adds depth and authenticity to his works. Lewis's vulnerability emanates from his willingness to grapple with profound existential questions and doubt. He fearlessly explores the complexities of faith, acknowledging his struggles and uncertainties along the way. His writings bear witness to a soul unafraid to confront the deepest recesses of his being, laying bare his vulnerabilities and allowing readers to connect with his humanity. Through his autobiographical works, such as "Surprised by Joy" and "A Grief Observed," Lewis bares his innermost thoughts and emotions, sharing subjective experiences of joy, loss, and profound grief. In these raw and honest reflections, he invites readers into his intimate journey, breaking down the barriers that often separate individuals and fostering empathy and understanding. Lewis's vulnerability also shines through his fictional characters. From the emotionally complex Digory Kirke in "The Magician's Nephew" to the tormented Ransom in the Space Trilogy, he infuses his creations with relatable human struggles and vulnerabilities. Through their experiences, Lewis offers readers a mirror to examine their vulnerabilities and navigate life and faith's complexities. Moreover, Lewis's vulnerability is evident in his willingness to express his deep longings and desires. He explores themes of love, hope, and the ache for transcendence in works like "The Four Loves" and "Till We Have Faces." He bears his longing for something beyond the material world, inviting readers to join him on a profound quest for meaning and fulfillment. In embracing vulnerability, Lewis asks us to embrace our humanity, with all its flaws, doubts, and longings. He reminds us that it is through embracing our vulnerabilities that we find connection, empathy, and growth. His vulnerability opens a doorway for authentic encounters, where masks can be shed and genuine transformation can occur. The enduring legacy of C.S. Lewis lies not only in his intellectual contributions but also in his vulnerable exploration of the human condition. His willingness to expose his doubts, struggles, and desires allows readers to engage with his writings on a deeply personal level. Through his vulnerability, he encourages us to embrace our abilities, fostering a deeper connection with ourselves, others, and the mysteries of faith and existence.

The vulnerability of John Chrysostom, the revered fourth-century Christian theologian, and preacher, illuminates the profound depths of his spiritual journey and the transformative power of his teachings. Beneath his influential rhetoric and spiritual authority lies a genuine openness and an authentic connection to human experience. Chrysostom's vulnerability manifests in his profound empathy and compassion for the struggles and suffering of others. In his sermons and writings, he addresses his time's social and moral issues with a raw sincerity that acknowledges the realities of human frailty and the world's complexities. He does not shy away from confronting injustice, speaking truth to power, and advocating for the marginalized, thus revealing the vulnerability of his own heart and his unwavering commitment to social justice. Chrysostom's vulnerability shines through his personal struggles and inner turmoil. In his writings, he reveals his battles with doubt, temptation, and the challenges of living a virtuous life. He does not present himself as a perfect figure but as someone who grapples with the human condition, seeking wisdom and transformation in his faith journey. Chrysostom's vulnerability also emerges in his candid self-reflection and repentance. He recognizes his shortcomings and sins, expressing genuine remorse and a profound desire for spiritual growth. His humility and willingness to acknowledge his imperfections provide a relatable example for others, encouraging them to embark on their paths of self-examination and repentance. Chrysostom's vulnerability finds expression in his connections and relationships. He genuinely cares for the spiritual well-being of his community and seeks to foster authentic relationships grounded in love and mutual support. He opens his heart to others, offering guidance, encouragement, and a listening ear, thus creating a space for vulnerability and emotional connection to flourish. As a member of the Coptic Church, I have received this saint's rich teachings and wisdom. The Coptic Church, with its rich traditions and deep-rooted history, has a significant connection to John Chrysostom. While John Chrysostom is often associated with the Byzantine Church, his influence extends beyond its boundaries, and his teachings have impacted various Christian denominations, including my church. The Coptic Church, one of the oldest Christian communities in the world, traces its roots back to the apostolic era in Egypt. Its theological foundation is grounded in the teachings of the early Church Fathers, including John Chrysostom. Although the Coptic Church developed its unique liturgical traditions and theological perspectives, it acknowledges the profound contributions of Chrysostom to the broader Christian tradition. John Chrysostom's theological and moral teachings resonate with the core principles of the Coptic Church. His emphasis on social justice, compassion, and care for the marginalized aligns with the Coptic Church's commitment to serving the community and advocating for the oppressed. His calls for humility, repentance, and spiritual growth resonate with my church's emphasis on asceticism and inner transformation. The church values the importance of liturgical worship and sacred rituals, which are central to Chrysostom's teachings. His profound understanding of the Eucharist and its significance as a transformative encounter with the divine mirrors the Coptic Church's reverence for the sacraments and their transformative power in the lives of believers. While theological and liturgical differences exist between the Byzantine and Coptic traditions, John Chrysostom's legacy has left an indelible mark on the broader Christian tradition, including the Coptic Church. His teachings continue to inspire and guide Coptic Christians in their faith, reinforcing their commitment to a life of holiness, social justice, and devotion to Christ.

In summary, John Chrysostom's influence transcends denominational boundaries, and his teachings have had a meaningful impact on the Coptic Church. Through his enduring legacy, Chrysostom continues to be celebrated as a beloved figure within the Coptic Church and a source of inspiration for its followers. Through his writings, he taught me to be vulnerable. In embracing vulnerability, Chrysostom models a spiritual path inviting others to embrace their vulnerabilities. He recognizes that true transformation and growth occur when we confront our weaknesses, acknowledge our limitations, and open ourselves to the transformative power of God's grace. His vulnerability creates a safe and nurturing environment for authentic encounters where individuals can connect with God and one another. The enduring impact of John Chrysostom lies not only in his profound theological insights and persuasive oratory but also in his vulnerable humanity. Through his willingness to reveal his struggles, doubts, and genuine care for others, he touches the hearts of generations. His vulnerability remains an inspiring reminder that the journey of faith encompasses the full spectrum of human experience and invites us all to embrace our vulnerabilities as catalysts for spiritual growth and authentic connections.

While "vulnerability" may not be explicitly mentioned in the Bible, several scriptures speak to the themes of openness, authenticity, and trust in God. These verses can guide us in understanding the importance of vulnerability in our relationship with God and others. Here are a few scriptures that touch upon these themes:

1. Psalm 51:17 - "My sacrifice, O God, is a broken spirit; a broken and contrite heart you, God, will not despise."
   Reflection: This verse reminds us that God values humility and an honest, open heart. We find His mercy and grace by acknowledging our brokenness and surrendering our vulnerabilities to God.

2. 2 Corinthians 12:9 - "But he said to me, 'My grace is sufficient for you, for my power is made perfect in weakness.' Therefore, I will gladly boast about my weaknesses so Christ's power may rest on me."
   Reflection: Here, the apostle Paul speaks of finding strength and power in weakness. Embracing our vulnerabilities allows us to rely on God's grace and experience His transformative work.

3. Proverbs 3:5-6 - "Trust in the LORD with all your heart and lean not on your understanding; in all your ways submit to him, and he will make your paths straight."

31

Reflection: This verse encourages us to trust God, surrender our need for control, and rely on His wisdom. It requires vulnerability to let go of our understanding and humbly submit to His guidance.

4. James 5:16 - "Therefore confess your sins to each other and pray for each other so that you may be healed. The prayer of a righteous person is powerful and effective."
    Reflection: Vulnerability plays a role in our relationships with others as well. This verse encourages us to confess our sins to one another, fostering an environment of openness, support, and accountability. We can find healing through vulnerability and experience the power of prayer in the community.

5. Ephesians 4:2 - "Be completely humble and gentle; be patient, bearing with one another in love."
    Reflection: This verse reminds us of the importance of vulnerability in our interactions with others. We create a safe space for open communication and authentic connection by approaching relationships with humility, gentleness, and patience.

While these scriptures may not explicitly mention vulnerability, they point us toward the principles and attitudes that underpin vulnerability—such as honesty, humility, trust, and openness. By embracing these qualities in our relationship with God and others, we can experience deeper connections, growth, and the transformative power of His love and grace.

Selah

Here are a few creative exercises on vulnerability:

1. Reflective Writing: Take out a journal or a blank sheet of paper. Set aside some uninterrupted time for reflection. Begin by pondering moments in your life where you have experienced vulnerability. It could be when you took a risk, shared your emotions, or allowed yourself to be seen authentically. Write about those experiences, exploring how vulnerability made you feel and what you learned from those moments. Be open and honest with yourself as you delve into these reflections.

2. Artistic Expression: Engage in a creative activity that allows you to express vulnerability visually. It could be painting, drawing, collaging, or any other artistic medium that resonates with you. As you create, focus on capturing the essence of vulnerability. Explore colors, textures, and symbols that represent the emotions and sensations associated with exposure. Let your artwork be a visual expression of your journey with vulnerability.

3. Guided Meditation: Find a quiet, comfortable space to sit or lie down. Close your eyes and take a few deep breaths to center yourself. Begin a guided meditation focused on vulnerability. Allow yourself to fully immerse yourself in the reflection, exploring the sensations and emotions within you. Embrace vulnerability in this safe and introspective space, and let meditation guide you toward a deeper understanding and acceptance of vulnerability within yourself.

4. Role-Playing: Enlist a trusted friend or family member to participate in a role-playing exercise. Choose a vulnerability scenario, such as sharing a personal struggle or expressing a deep fear. Take turns playing the roles of the vulnerable person and the supportive listener. Practice representing vulnerability authentically and offering empathy and support to each other. This exercise can help you develop a sense of compassion and enhance your ability to create safe spaces for vulnerability in real-life situations.

5. Group Sharing: Gather a small group of trusted friends or peers open to exploring vulnerability together. Create a safe and non-judgmental space for everyone to share their experiences and feelings about vulnerability. Encourage each person to share a story, poem, or artwork representing their vulnerability. Engage in a supportive and compassionate discussion, offering reflections and insights to one another. This exercise fosters connection and reminds us that vulnerability is a shared human experience.

Remember, vulnerability can be challenging but holds immense transformative power. Approach these exercises with an open heart and mind, allowing yourself to lean into vulnerability and explore its depths. We can cultivate deeper connections, personal growth, and a greater sense of authenticity by embracing vulnerability.

THIS IS YOUR PERSONAL SPACE

WRITE HOW YOU WILL

REFRESH, ESCAPE, SOOTHE, TRANQUILIZE

·LeT·
yourself
-REST-

DATE:

_____   _____
_____   _____
_____   _____
_____   _____
_____   _____
_____   _____
_____   _____
_____   _____
_____   _____
_____   _____

I WILL REST TODAY BY...

_____
_____
_____
_____
_____
_____

CHAPTER 4

Cultivating Self-Compassion

IN A WORLD that often celebrates achievement, success, and criticism, self-compassion is a gentle yet powerful force, offering healing and profound transformation. It is the art of extending the same kindness, understanding, and love to us that we readily provide to others. Fostering the practice invites us to grip our imperfections, heal our wounds, and nourish our souls. In this journey of self-discovery, we unlock the key to living a radiant and fulfilling life. Self-compassion begins with a fundamental shift in perspective—a change that incorporates the imperfect beauty within. Instead of harshly judging ourselves for our flaws and shortcomings, we learn to view them as part of our uniqueness. We recognize that imperfection is the fertile ground for growth and authenticity. Through it, we gently cradle our vulnerabilities, acknowledging that they are not weaknesses but threads that connect us to our shared humanity. Accepting our imperfections opens the door to self-love, paving the way for a life of self-compassion, growth, and learning. Central to cultivating self-compassion is the gift of radical self-acceptance. It is the conscious choice to embrace ourselves fully, without conditions or reservations. We liberate ourselves from self-judgment and criticism, allowing our hearts to open wide in unconditional love. With each step on this transformative path, we come face to face with our shadows, our past mistakes, and our perceived inadequacies. Yet, through self-compassion, we find the courage to forgive ourselves, heal, and nurture the seeds of self-acceptance. In doing so, we blossom into the fullest expression of our authentic selves.

Within us resides an inner child—a vulnerable, innocent essence that longs for tender care and compassion. We must connect with this tender part of ourselves, listen to its needs, and respond with unwavering love. As we embrace our inner child, we acknowledge the wounds it carries and provide the comfort and support it longs for. We heal the wounds of the past and create a nurturing environment where our inner child can thrive. In this profound act of self-care, we reclaim our innocence, rediscover our joy, and tend to a deep wellspring of compassion that extends to every aspect of our lives. Self-compassion and personal growth share an intricate dance intertwined in a harmonious embrace. It is through the lens of self-compassion that we dare to step into the unknown, take risks, and explore our true potential. We recognize that growth is a self-discovery journey marked by triumphs and setbacks. We find the resilience to learn from our mistakes, nurture ourselves through challenges, and celebrate our victories. With each step on this growth path, self-compassion becomes our guiding light, empowering us to embrace our authenticity and unleash our limitless potential. Ingraining self-compassion is a transformative voyage, an act of radical self-love that unfolds the fullness of our being. Self-compassion is not a solitary endeavor but an invitation to foster compassion in our relationships. As we fill our hearts with compassion, we naturally radiate that warmth and empathy to those around us. We become beacons of understanding, creating a flow that touches the lives of others and produces a more compassionate world. In this transformative quest of encouraging self-compassion, you must embrace the profound truth that you are worthy of love, gentleness, and acceptance. As you nurture the garden of your heart, you will witness the blossoming of gifts of inner peace, resilience, and a deep sense of belonging. Embrace the power within you to be kind to yourself, to hold yourself with tenderness, and to unleash the extraordinary potential that self-compassion brings.

Self-compassion can rewire our minds, reshaping our thought patterns and fostering a more positive and nurturing inner landscape. By consistently practicing it, we begin rewiring the neural pathways within our brains. First, self-compassion interrupts the habitual patterns of self-criticism and self-judgment that often dominate our thoughts. It encourages us to approach ourselves with kindness and understanding, creating new pathways that replace self-critical thoughts with self-acceptance and self-care. Over time, these new pathways become stronger and more ingrained, shifting our overall mindset. It activates regions of the brain associated with positive emotions and well-being. It stimulates the release of oxytocin, often called the "love hormone," which promotes feelings of connection, contentment, and calm. This neurochemical response reinforces the rewiring process, strengthening the neural ties associated with self-compassion and positive self-regard. It helps regulate our stress response. It activates the prefrontal cortex, the part of the brain responsible for executive functions and emotional regulation, which helps dampen the amygdala's response to stress and negative emotions.

This rewiring process allows us to navigate challenges and setbacks with greater resilience and equanimity. In addition, practicing self-compassion enhances our overall self-awareness. It encourages us to observe our thoughts and emotions without judgment, fostering a sense of mindfulness and self-reflection. This increased self-awareness allows us to identify and challenge self-limiting beliefs and negative thought patterns, humanizing a more empowering inner dialogue. As we continue to engage in self-compassion practices, the rewiring of our minds becomes more pronounced. The new neural pathways strengthen, creating a foundation of resilience. This rewiring leads to a more positive and compassionate mindset, transforming how we perceive ourselves, relate to others, and navigate life's difficulties.

Enhancing our self-awareness is a powerful daily reminder to check in with ourselves. Self-awareness is an endearing trait that refers to the ability of individuals to introspectively recognize and understand their emotions, beliefs, and behaviors. It involves being conscious of oneself as a separate and unique individual with distinct characteristics, desires, and motivations. Self-awareness is significant in personal growth, relationships, and overall well-being. By being aware of our strengths, weaknesses, and areas for improvement, we can actively enhance our skills, overcome limitations, and achieve our goals. It helps us recognize behavior patterns, understand reactions, and make more informed choices. Self-awareness is intricately linked to emotional intelligence, which involves managing emotions and understanding and empathizing with the feelings of others. By being self-aware, we can better understand the impact of our feelings on our thoughts and actions, leading to improved self-regulation and better interpersonal relationships. It enables individuals to express themselves more effectively. By understanding our thoughts, beliefs, and values, we can communicate them clearly and assertively. Additionally, awareness of our emotions allows us to speak appropriately, leading to better interpersonal communication and conflict resolution. Self-awareness helps individuals understand their authentic selves—their true values, passions, and aspirations. By aligning our actions with our authentic selves, we can lead more fulfilling lives and experience a greater sense of purpose. It also enhances self-confidence as we become more aware of our strengths and embrace our uniqueness. When self-aware, we are more conscious of our values, motivations, and biases, which influence our decision-making process. Self-awareness helps us make choices aligned with our long-term goals, deals, and ideological principles, leading to more consistent and fulfilling decision-making outcomes. Self-awareness is valuable because it promotes personal growth, emotional intelligence, effective communication, authenticity, confidence, better decision-making, and improved relationships. Developing self-awareness is an ongoing process that involves introspection, reflection, and feedback from others, and it can enhance various aspects of our lives.

One real-life example of self-compassion and self-awareness that many people can relate to is the journey of Brené Brown, a renowned researcher and author specializing in topics such as vulnerability, shame, and resilience. Brené Brown's work and firsthand experiences offer valuable insights into the power of self-compassion and self-awareness. Brené Brown's journey began when she embarked on extensive research to understand vulnerability, shame, and human connection. Through her research, she gained profound insights into the importance of self-compassion and self-awareness in leading a wholehearted and fulfilling life. She discovered that self-compassion plays a vital role in navigating vulnerability and shame. She learned to embrace her imperfections and treat herself with kindness and understanding. Instead of being overly self-critical, she cultivated self-compassion by acknowledging her struggles, accepting her mistakes, and providing herself with the empathy and support she would offer a loved one. Throughout her research, Brené Brown developed a deep sense of self-awareness. She recognized her terms of perfectionism and fear of vulnerability, holding her back from living a wholehearted life. By becoming aware of these patterns, she could challenge and overcome them. This self-awareness allowed her to understand her triggers, confront her limiting beliefs, and make conscious choices aligned with her values. Her journey exemplifies the transformative power of self-compassion and self-awareness. Through her research and individual experiences, she has inspired countless individuals to cultivate these qualities in their own lives. Her vulnerability and openness about her struggles have resonated with people, fostering a sense of connection and providing a relatable example for others to learn from. By embracing self-compassion and practicing self-awareness, Brené Brown has been able to transform her own life and, in turn, impact the lives of many others.

Brené Brown was born on November 18, 1965, in San Antonio, Texas. Brown obtained her bachelor's degree in social work from the University of Texas at Austin. She later pursued a Master of Social Work (MSW) degree and a Ph.D. in Social Work from the University of Houston Graduate College of Social Work. Her interest in studying vulnerability, courage, and connection topics stemmed from her struggles and experiences. As a researcher, she delved into understanding human emotions, particularly shame, exposure, and openness. Brown's work has profoundly impacted psychology, self-help, leadership, and personal development. One of her most significant breakthroughs came with her 2010 TED Talk titled "The Power of Vulnerability," which became one of the most viewed TED Talks ever. In her talk, Brown shared her insights and research findings about embracing vulnerability to cultivate deeper connections, empathy, and resilience. Following the success of her TED Talk, Brown published several best-selling books, including "Daring Greatly: How the Courage to Be Vulnerable Transforms the Way We Live, Love, Parent, and Lead" (2012), "Rising Strong: How the Ability to Reset Transforms the Way We Live, Love, Parent, and Lead" (2015), and "Braving the Wilderness: The Quest for True Belonging and the Courage to Stand Alone" (2017). These books further explore themes of vulnerability, shame, resilience, and the power of embracing one's authentic self. Brené Brown's work has garnered widespread recognition and has been influential in helping individuals, organizations, and communities embrace vulnerability, develop empathy, and foster meaningful connections. Her storytelling style and relatable examples have resonated with people from various backgrounds, making her work accessible and impactful across different audiences. She is one of countless examples of someone who turned her pain into gain. Because of her, people today are taking great strides to extend compassion to themselves and become more aware of themselves. I encourage you to read her materials and listen to her podcasts.

God's infinite love encompasses a profound desire to promote self-compassion and release the burden of self-judgment. In His divine wisdom, God recognizes that our well-being extends beyond physical health, encompassing the realms of our hearts and minds. He beckons us to treat ourselves with the same compassion and grace that He showers upon us. God pleas that we value our inner selves, refining a gentle and sustaining attitude towards our beings. He longs for us to release the chains of self-judgment, embrace our imperfections, and acknowledge our worthiness. God's ultimate intention is for us to live healthy lives in the physical sense and the realms of our emotions and thoughts. By embracing self-compassion and letting go of self-judgment, we align ourselves with God's divine plan for our well-being, embracing a path of wholeness and true, transformative health. Recognizing and acknowledging the role of God provides a sense of liberation and freedom from condemning our mistakes. Believing in a forgiving and compassionate higher power can offer reassurance when we make mistakes. Many religious and spiritual traditions emphasize the concept of divine forgiveness, teaching that sincere repentance and seeking forgiveness can lead to redemption and renewal. This understanding can alleviate self-condemnation and inspire personal growth. Recognizing that we are fallible human beings and that our imperfections are part of our shared human experience can foster humility. Believing in the transformative power of God helps us accept our mistakes as opportunities for growth rather than sources of shame. This perspective encourages self-compassion and allows us to approach our errors with a desire to learn and improve. The belief in a guiding force provides a source of wisdom and strength during times of difficulty. By seeking guidance and relying on Him, individuals may find comfort in the idea that they are not alone in their journey of self-improvement. This belief can instill hope and resilience, enabling individuals to overcome their mistakes with purpose. The belief in a divine power that can change and transform individuals can be empowering. Rather than dwelling on past mistakes, recognizing the potential for growth and transformation allows us to focus on becoming the best version of ourselves. Faith in a higher power often fosters a sense of community and belonging. Being part of a religious or spiritual community provides support, encouragement, and opportunities for mutual learning and growth. Sharing experiences, including mistakes, within a supportive community can further alleviate self-condemnation and facilitate personal development.

Selah

Visualize and Create

Create a beautiful coloring page depicting the essence of self-compassion and personal growth. In the center, draw a graceful figure representing a person with flowing lines and gentle curves. The figure radiates warmth and serenity, symbolizing self-compassion. The arms of the figure gracefully reach outward, embracing and intertwining with vibrant, blooming vines.

The vines, representing personal growth, are adorned with delicate flowers and leaves, each unique and flourishing. These intricate vines weave around the figure, symbolizing the interconnectedness of self-compassion and personal growth. The colors of the flowers and leaves can be varied, representing the diverse experiences and transformations that occur on the journey of personal growth.

Within the figure's silhouette, incorporate intricate patterns or mandala-like designs, representing the internal growth and self-reflection that occur on the path of self-compassion. These patterns can be soothing and complex, encouraging a meditative coloring experience.

As you color this picture, let your imagination guide you. Use a palette of soothing hues, such as soft blues, gentle greens, and warm earth tones, to evoke a sense of tranquility and growth. Allow the colors to flow harmoniously, blending and intertwining, mirroring the dance between self-compassion and personal development.

Remember, coloring can be a meditative practice, offering a moment of self-care and mindfulness. As you color, immerse yourself in the beauty of the design, reflecting on the profound words that inspired it. Let your creativity and inner wisdom guide your hand as you bring this meaningful picture to life, embracing the intricate dance of self-compassion and personal growth.

If art is not your love language, explore another reflective method:

1. Journaling: Grab a journal or a blank sheet of paper and find a quiet space to reflect without distractions. Begin by writing down your thoughts and feelings about self-compassion. Explore any barriers or resistance you may have towards extending compassion to yourself. Write freely and honestly, allowing your ideas to flow without judgment. Consider questions like: How do you currently treat yourself when facing challenges or setbacks? Are there any patterns of self-criticism or harsh judgment that you notice? How do you think practicing self-compassion could impact your overall well-being and growth?

2. Self-Reflection: Find a comfortable and peaceful spot where you can engage in self-reflection. Close your eyes, take a few deep breaths, and allow your mind to settle. Consider a recent situation or experience where you felt self-critical or lacked self-compassion. Without judgment, observe the thoughts, emotions, and physical sensations that arise. Notice any patterns or recurring themes in how you tend to treat

yourself. As you follow these patterns, gently remind yourself that self-compassion is essential to personal growth and well-being. Reflect on how extending self-compassion in that situation might have changed your experience or response.

3. Affirmations: Create a set of self-compassionate affirmations that resonate with you. These can be positive statements or reminders that foster a kind and compassionate attitude toward yourself. Examples include: "I deserve love and kindness, including from myself," "I acknowledge my mistakes and learn from them without judgment," or "I am worthy of self-care and self-compassion." Write down these affirmations and place them somewhere visible, such as a mirror or your workspace. Repeat them regularly as a reminder to treat yourself with compassion.

4. Gratitude Practice: Cultivating gratitude can be a powerful tool in fostering self-compassion. Take a few moments each day to reflect on three things you are grateful for about yourself. These can be qualities, achievements, or actions you appreciate and value in yourself. Allow yourself to fully experience gratitude and let it wash over you, acknowledging your worth and strengths. This practice can help shift your focus from self-criticism to self-appreciation and compassion.

5. Seek Support: Remember that self-compassion is a journey, and it can be helpful to seek support from others. Reach out to trusted friends, family members, or professionals who can provide a safe space for you to explore and deepen your self-compassion practice. Please share your experiences, challenges, and insights with them, and allow their perspectives and support to enrich your journey.

Remember, practicing self-compassion is an ongoing process that requires patience and self-awareness. These reflective exercises can deepen your understanding of self-compassion and its transformative potential.

THIS IS YOUR PERSONAL SPACE

WRITE HOW YOU WILL

REFRESH, ESCAPE, SOOTHE, TRANQUILIZE

Let Yourself REST

DATE:

I WILL REST TODAY BY...

CHAPTER 5

Nurturing Inner Joy

FROM THE ASHES of shame, we emerge resilient and determined to embark on a path of healing and self-discovery. As we navigate this journey, we realize that within our being lies a profound desire for joy—a yearning to experience a sense of inner contentment that transcends the external world. In nurturing this inner joy, we find the power to transform our lives and reclaim our inherent happiness. To embark on this transformative journey, we must first recognize that joy is not solely dependent on external circumstances. It is not a fleeting emotion accompanying the ebb and flow of life's challenges. True joy is a persistent presence within us, awaiting our acknowledgment and nurturing. It is a state of being that can be cultivated through intentional practices and a shift in perspective. To nurture inner joy, we must begin by shifting our perspectives. We train our minds to focus on the positives, finding gratitude in the smallest moments. We let go of the weight of comparison and embrace our unique journey. We understand that joy resides not in the destination but in the beauty of the present moment. By shifting our focus to the blessings surrounding us, we pave the way for joy to flourish. Practicing mindfulness plays a pivotal role in this journey. As we engage fully in the present moment, we awaken to the richness of life's gifts. We savor the simple pleasures—the warmth of the sun on our skin, the gentle caress of a loved one's hand, the melody of laughter. Through mindfulness, we enrich a deep appreciation for the here and now, opening our hearts to the abundant joy within and around us. We recognize that growth and transformation are not linear but filled with twists, turns, and unexpected detours. In these moments, we find opportunities for growth and joy. We release the need for perfection and allow ourselves to revel in the imperfections that make our journey uniquely ours. It is through embracing the entirety of our experience—the joys, the challenges, and everything in between—that we discover the profound depth of inner joy. It requires intentional practices that nourish the soul. We explore activities that bring us immense joy and prioritize them in our lives. It could be engaging in creative pursuits, spending time in nature, practicing self-care, or connecting with loved ones. These practices fill our cups and create space for joy to flourish and radiate outward. Gratitude becomes an anchor for our joy-filled existence. We cultivate a daily gratitude practice, consciously acknowledging the blessings that grace our lives. In expressing gratitude, we shift our focus from lack to abundance, amplifying the joy that permeates our being. We become aware of the interconnectedness of joy and gratitude and their profound ability to transform our perspective and nurture our inner well-being.

Happiness and joy, while often used interchangeably, possess distinct qualities and nuances. Happiness is a transient and fleeting emotional state characterized by a sense of contentment, pleasure, or satisfaction derived from external circumstances or events. It is often tied to specific experiences, achievements, or favorable conditions. Happiness can be influenced by external factors such as relationships, material possessions, or accomplishments, and its intensity may vary over time. On the other hand, joy is a deep and lasting sense of inner gladness, contentment, and fulfillment that transcends external circumstances. Unlike happiness, joy emanates from within and is not dependent on external factors. It arises from a connection to something greater than us. Joy is more enduring and resilient, not easily diminished by temporary setbacks or unfavorable conditions. While happiness can be momentary and tied to specific events, joy encompasses a deeper, more sustained state of well-being and inner contentment. It often arises from gratitude, acceptance, and alignment with one's values and purpose. Joy can coexist with other emotions, including sadness or pain, as it is not solely dependent on external circumstances. Happiness is a transient emotional state influenced by external factors, while joy is a deeper and more profound state of inner contentment and fulfillment that emanates from within. Both experiences hold value in our lives, but joy offers a lasting and resilient sense of well-being that transcends life's difficulties.

The impact of joy on rewiring our minds is significant and transformative. When we experience true happiness, it has the power to reconfigure our neural pathways, fostering a more positive and resilient mindset. Joy activates the brain's reward centers, releasing a cascade of neurochemicals, such as dopamine, serotonin, and endorphins. These chemicals generate pleasure and happiness and contribute to the rewiring process. As we repeatedly experience joy, these neural pathways become strengthened and more easily accessible, creating a predisposition towards positive emotions and a greater capacity for resilience. Joy promotes a state of openness and curiosity, facilitating cognitive flexibility and creativity. When we are filled with joy, our minds are more receptive to innovative ideas and perspectives. This openness encourages us to explore different possibilities and engage in creative problem-solving, enhancing our cognitive capacities. Joy rewires our attentional patterns, directing our focus toward the abundance and beauty around us. This shift in attention helps counteract the brain's natural negativity bias, reducing the impact of negative thoughts and promoting a more positive outlook. Additionally, joy fosters a sense of connection and social bonding. When we experience pleasure, it activates brain regions associated with empathy, compassion, and social harmony. This rewiring leads to enhanced relationships and a greater sense of belonging, contributing to overall well-being and mental health. Over time, the repeated experience of joy and its associated rewiring processes can lead to lasting changes in the brain. These changes result in a more positive cognitive framework, increased resilience in the face of challenges, and a greater capacity to find joy in everyday life. Happiness becomes a foundational aspect of our mindset, shaping our perceptions, attitudes, and responses to the world around us. Rewiring our minds through fun opens the door to greater emotional well-being, cognitive flexibility, gratitude, social connection, and overall resilience. By cultivating and embracing joy in our lives, we can actively shape our neural pathways, fostering a positive and resilient mindset that allows us to thrive and flourish.

In the quest for lasting joy, we discover a truth that transcends the world's fleeting pleasures: true happiness is found in Christ. He is the wellspring from which unshakable delight flows, offering a joy that surpasses circumstances and endures through all seasons of life. Through a deep and intimate relationship with Him, we can unearth true happiness, transforming our hearts and infusing every aspect of our existence with profound meaning and purpose. In Christ, we encounter the ultimate source of joy—the gift of salvation. As we embrace His sacrifice on the cross and accept His love and forgiveness, we are freed from the weight of sin and the burden of guilt. The assurance of eternal life and reconciliation with God fills our hearts with joy that cannot be extinguished. This foundational joy in our salvation becomes the anchor amidst life's storms, bringing comfort and hope even amid trials. Abiding in the presence of Christ is the path to deep joy. We must practice staying in His company daily to find enduring happiness in Christ. We develop a vibrant relationship with Him through prayer, worship, and studying His Word. As we draw near to Him, He draws near to us, unveiling the depths of His love and filling our hearts with a joy that surpasses understanding. In His presence, we discover a refuge of peace and a wellspring of delight that sustains us through life's challenges. In surrendering our will to Christ and aligning our lives with His purposes, we experience a joy that springs from obedience. As we yield to His guidance, we find that His plans for us far exceed our limited understanding. Walking in His ways, we discover fulfillment, meaning, and a deep sense of purpose that brings joy. True joy is not found in pursuing our desires but in wholeheartedly pursuing the will of our loving Creator.

As we allow Christ to transform us from the inside out, we experience the joy of becoming more like Him. Through the work of the Holy Spirit within us, we are conformed to His image, reflecting His love, kindness, and compassion. This transformation brings joy as we witness the fruit of the Spirit blossoming in our lives—love, joy, peace, patience, kindness, goodness, faithfulness, gentleness, and self-control. The joy of growing in Christlikeness is a testament to His transformative power and a source of inspiration for others. The joy we find in Christ is not meant to be kept to ourselves but shared with the world. As we witness His love, grace, and redemption, we become agents of joy, reflecting His light to those around us. By sharing the Good News of salvation and pointing others to the abundant joy found in Christ, we fulfill His purpose and experience the multiplied joy that comes from seeing lives transformed by His grace. In Christ, you have access to a joy that transcends circumstances, surpasses understanding, and endures through all seasons of life. Through salvation, abiding in His presence, surrendering to His will, growing in Christlikeness, and sharing His joy, you can experience a profound and unshakable delight found only in Him. As we wholeheartedly embrace nurturing inner joy, we witness a transformation within ourselves. The seeds of joy once buried deep within us bloom into a vibrant garden of happiness. We radiate an infectious pleasure that touches the lives of those around us, creating a ripple effect of positivity and inspiration. In nurturing our inner joy, we rediscover our authentic selves. We embrace our strengths and weaknesses, knowing they are all part of our beautiful tapestry. We release the shackles of shame and step into the freedom of self-acceptance and self-love. From this place of authenticity and joy, we become beacons of light, illuminating the path for others to find their inner joy. This path to finding such pleasure is not for the fainthearted.

One of the greatest oxymorons from the Bible is the passage from James 1:2-3, "Consider it pure joy, my brothers and sisters, whenever you face trials of many kinds because you know that the testing of your faith produces perseverance."

This passage can indeed seem paradoxical or contradictory. It suggests finding joy amid challenging circumstances or trials.

However, it is important to understand this statement's underlying message and context. James does not mean we should feel happy about the trials, as they often involve pain, hardship, or difficulties. Rather, he encourages believers to have a perspective beyond immediate circumstances and approach trials with faith and perseverance. The "joy" referred to here is not a superficial or fleeting emotion based on temporary events but a deeper sense of inner peace and steadfastness. It is a recognition that trials can serve a purpose in our spiritual growth and development and that our faith can be assessed and strengthened through them. James highlights the transformative nature of problems, explaining that they produce perseverance, which is the ability to endure and remain steadfast in facing challenges. By enduring trials with a mindset of faith and determination, believers can grow in character, wisdom, and spiritual maturity. While it may still appear paradoxical, this passage invites individuals to shift their perspective and find meaning and purpose amid trials, understanding that they can contribute to personal growth and deepening one's faith.

One inspiring example of a woman in the Bible who demonstrated joy amidst trials is the prophet and judge, Deborah. Deborah's story is found in the Book of Judges in the Old Testament. Deborah was a judge and a spiritual leader during oppression and conflict in ancient Israel. She faced the challenge of leading her people, the Israelites, to victory against their enemies, the Canaanites, who had oppressed them for years. Despite the challenging circumstances and the weight of leadership on her shoulders, Deborah exuded a sense of confidence, courage, and joy. In Judges 5:1-3, Deborah and Barak, the military leader she appointed, sing a joyful song of praise to God after their victory over the Canaanites. This song, known as the "Song of Deborah," reflects her joy and gratitude for God's faithfulness and the liberation of her people. Deborah's joy stemmed from her unwavering faith in God and trust in His plans. She believed that God would guide and empower her in fulfilling her role as a judge and leader. Deborah's leadership and the joy she exuded inspired those around her, leading to peace and prosperity for the Israelites. Deborah's example highlights the power of pleasure amid trials. Despite the challenging circumstances and the responsibility she carried, she chose to focus on God's faithfulness and express her gratitude through joyful praise. Her story inspires all people, encouraging us to find joy and strength in our faith, trust God's plans, and maintain a positive outlook even when faced with inconvenient situations.

Selah

1. Joyful Memories: Recall moments when you experienced pure joy. Close your eyes and transport yourself back to those times. Visualize the details, the emotions, and the sensations associated with those joyful memories. Write them down in your journal, capturing the essence of those moments. Reflect on what made those experiences so joyful and how you can recreate similar moments of joy in your present life.

2. Core Values and Alignment: Reflect on your core values—the principles and beliefs that guide your life. Consider whether your current lifestyle, choices, and pursuits align with those values. Identify areas where misalignment may lead to a lack of joy or fulfillment. Ponder ways to realign your life with your core values, bringing more fun and authenticity into your daily experiences.

3. Joy-Inducing Activities: List activities or hobbies that consistently bring you joy. Reflect on why these activities bring you happiness and how to incorporate them. Consider whether there are any new activities or pursuits you would like to explore that have the potential to ignite joy within you. Write down actionable steps to incorporate these joy-inducing activities into your routine.

4. Intentional Mindfulness: Engage in a mindful breathing exercise, focusing on the present moment. Breathe deeply and slowly, observing the sensation of the breath entering and leaving your body. With each breath, consciously release any tension, worries, or negativity, inviting joy to fill your being. Practice being fully present now, savoring the simple pleasures, and finding joy in the beauty surrounding you.

5. Commit to Joyful Living: Commit to prioritizing joy as you conclude your reflective exercise. Set an intention to seek out and create moments of joy each day. Embrace a positive mindset, nurture gratitude, and cultivate a positive perspective. Challenge yourself to let go of negativity, embrace simplicity, and celebrate the blessings that come your way.

Remember, this reflective exercise is a personal journey, and each person's path to joy is unique. Take the time to engage with these reflections regularly, allowing joy to become an intentional and integral part of your daily life. May this exercise guide you toward a deeper understanding and experience of joy, bringing fulfillment, contentment, and a renewed zest for life!

THIS IS YOUR PERSONAL SPACE

WRITE HOW YOU WILL

REFRESH, ESCAPE, SOOTHE, TRANQUILIZE

LET.
Yourself
-REST-

DATE:

I WILL REST TODAY BY...

CHAPTER 6

From Pain to Purpose

IN THE DEPTHS of our brokenness, there lies an extraordinary power—the power of resilience. It is within our capacity to rise above adversity, find strength in our vulnerabilities, and transform our pain into purpose. This chapter will explore the profound journey of resilience and transformation, discovering the untapped potential within our brokenness. Through this transformative process, we will uncover the meaning and purpose that can arise from our experiences of pain and hardship and learn how to channel our brokenness into personal growth and service to others. Resilience is a multifaceted concept that holds great significance in our lives. It encompasses adapting, persevering, and maintaining emotional strength in adversity. It goes beyond mere toughness or bouncing back—it involves a deep-rooted inner strength that enables us to withstand life's challenges with grace. By understanding the core components of resilience, including adaptability, perseverance, and emotional stability, we can support these qualities within ourselves. Resilience is a crucial skill to develop from an early age. Children and adolescents can be taught strategies to build resilience, enabling them to navigate life's challenges more effectively. Key factors contributing to resilience in young individuals include a nurturing environment, positive parenting, and school-based interventions. By empowering young people to develop healthy coping mechanisms, critical thinking skills, and emotional regulation, we equip them with tools to thrive in adversity. Developing personal resilience begins with prioritizing self-care. By taking care of our physical, emotional, and mental well-being, we build a sturdy foundation for strength. Practicing self-compassion and developing a growth mindset helps us approach challenges positively and adaptively. Mindfulness and relaxation techniques allow us to manage stress, enhance emotional stability, and find inner calm. Resilient individuals serve as powerful sources of inspiration and learning. By examining their stories and experiences, we can extract valuable lessons and strategies to apply in our own lives. We often find commonalities among resilient individuals, such as a powerful sense of purpose, optimism, and adaptability. By drawing inspiration from historical figures, celebrities, or personal role models who have exhibited resilience, we discover the diverse paths that stability can take and are encouraged to cultivate these qualities within ourselves.

One biblical character who exemplifies resilience is the apostle Paul. Paul faced numerous challenges throughout his life, including persecution, imprisonment, and physical ailments. Despite these hardships, he demonstrated remarkable resilience and unwavering faith in God. Paul's story offers valuable lessons for us on cultivating resilience in the face of adversity. One of the key aspects of Paul's strength was his unwavering commitment to his purpose and calling. He faced intense opposition and hostility for his beliefs, yet he remained steadfast in his mission to spread the gospel and build Christian communities. His deep sense of purpose fueled his resilience, enabling him to endure suffering and setbacks without losing sight of his mission. From Paul, we learn the importance of finding and embracing our purpose, as it gives us the strength and resilience needed to persevere in adversity. Paul's stability was also rooted in his unshakable faith in God. Despite his hardships, he consistently relied on God's strength, guidance, and provision. He trusted in God's faithfulness and believed that God's power was made perfect in his weakness. This unwavering faith sustained him through trials and enabled him to see beyond his circumstances. From Paul, we learn the transformative power of faith and the importance of cultivating a deep and intimate relationship with God, as it strengthens our resilience and allows us to find hope and purpose in even the most challenging situations. Furthermore, Paul demonstrated strength by embracing a mindset of gratitude and contentment. He found joy and peace in all circumstances, even amid adversity. He learned the secret of being content in any situation, whether in abundance or need. Paul's ability to find gratitude and contentment in every circumstance illustrates the power of perspective and its impact on our resilience. It reminds us to focus on our blessings rather than dwelling on the challenges and cultivate a gratitude mindset that helps us navigate hardships with resilience and grace. Paul's strength was marked by his willingness to seek support and community. Despite being independent and strong-willed, he recognized the importance of relying on others for encouragement, prayer, and support. He surrounded himself with like-minded believers who provided him with strength and encouragement. Paul's example teaches us the value of seeking help from others during challenging times, as it fosters resilience and reminds us that we are not alone in our struggles.

The life of the apostle Paul serves as a powerful example of resilience in the face of adversity. We can learn valuable lessons on cultivating resilience from his unwavering commitment to his purpose, deep faith in God, gratitude and contentment, and willingness to seek support. By embracing these principles, we can navigate life's challenges with strength, grace, and unwavering faith, just as Paul did. We can apply these principles in every aspect of life, even the workplace. Work can be challenging, and resilience is pivotal in navigating professional hurdles. By developing strength, we can overcome setbacks, manage stress, and adapt to changing circumstances. Resilience within organizations fosters a culture of support and provides employees with the tools to thrive amidst challenges. Strategies such as work-life balance, stress management, and fostering positive relationships build workplace resilience. Resilience extends to our relationships, influencing how we navigate conflicts and challenges. We cultivate trust, empathy, and effective communication by fostering resilient relationships. Resilient individuals prioritize emotional intelligence, active listening, and understanding within their relationships. Building social support networks and nurturing connectedness are vital in promoting resilience in our interactions. Stability is especially crucial in the face of trauma and adversity. Individuals who have experienced trauma can harness the strength to heal and rebuild their lives. Understanding the impact of adverse childhood experiences and their effects on resilience allows us to address and overcome trauma-related challenges. Seeking professional help, utilizing trauma-focused interventions, and embracing post-traumatic growth enable individuals to heal, find strength, and cultivate resilience.

Reading about the lives of others serves as a powerful source of encouragement and heart-filling inspiration for me. One impactful example of someone who embodies resilience and triumphs over struggle is Malvika Iyer. Malvika's life took an unexpected turn at age 13 when she survived a devastating bomb blast accident that resulted in the amputation of both her hands and severe injuries to her legs. However, she refused to let her circumstances define her. Despite her physical and emotional trauma, Malvika displayed extraordinary resilience and determination. She not only completed her education but went on to earn a Ph.D. in Social Work, specializing in disability rights and inclusivity. Malvika advocated for accessibility, inclusivity, and empowerment for persons with disabilities. As a motivational speaker, Malvika has inspired countless individuals with her powerful message of resilience, acceptance, and the importance of embracing one's abilities. She has delivered TED talks and shared her story at international forums, challenging societal stereotypes and inspiring others to break free from limitations. Malvika's resilience extends beyond her journey. Her work has brought attention to creating a more inclusive society with equal opportunities to thrive. Furthermore, Malvika is a beacon of hope for survivors of trauma and adversity. Her story is a testament to the human spirit's capacity to overcome challenges and find new purpose and meaning in life. In recognition of her remarkable achievements, Malvika has received numerous awards and accolades for her contributions to disability rights and social work. She inspires and empowers others through her advocacy, reminding us all that resilience and determination can transform lives and create a more inclusive and compassionate world.

Anyone has the potential to turn their pain into purpose. Adversity and pain facilitate personal growth, transformation, and the discovery of one's life purpose. When individuals navigate their pain and challenges, they often gain unique insights, resilience, and empathy that can be channeled into a meaningful sense. By reflecting on their experiences, finding meaning in their struggles, and seeking healing and growth, individuals can harness the power of their pain to impact their own lives and the lives of others positively. Transforming pain into purpose may involve various paths, such as advocacy, mentorship, creative expression, or community service. For example, someone who has experienced loss or illness may dedicate their efforts to supporting others facing similar challenges, becoming a source of comfort and guidance. Others may use their pain as inspiration to create art, music, or literature that uplifts and inspires others in similar circumstances. It is important to note that turning pain into purpose is a personal and unique journey. The process may require self-reflection, self-compassion, and seeking support from others. It can involve introspection, exploring one's values, passions, and strengths, and aligning them with a cause or mission that resonates deeply. While pain itself does not guarantee purpose, it is through the intentional and conscious exploration of our pain, coupled with a desire to be effective, that purpose can emerge. By embracing vulnerability, finding meaning in our experiences, and channeling our pain toward positive action, we can transform our lives and contribute to the greater good. It is important to remember that everyone's journey is unique, and turning pain into purpose may take time and patience. However, with resilience, self-reflection, and a willingness to grow, anyone can find purpose and meaning from their pain, using it for personal transformation and positively impacting the world.

In the realm of unsung heroes, my previous book, "The Beginning Starts at the End," highlights the remarkable story of my brother John. Although he may not have achieved fame as a celebrity, his impact on countless individuals facing addiction was immeasurable. Overcoming his struggles, John dedicated himself to providing hope and support to those who had lost their way. His selfless work touched the lives of many, demonstrating that one's influence and ability to make a positive impact extend far beyond fame and recognition. But it is important to recognize and appreciate celebrities who step out boldly and use their struggles to help others. Many well-known figures have used their platforms and firsthand experiences to raise awareness, inspire change, and support various causes. These individuals often face unique challenges due to their public visibility and the scrutiny that comes with fame. Despite these pressures, some celebrities have shared their struggles to help others in similar situations. Speaking openly about their experiences, they break down barriers, reduce stigma, and encourage individuals to seek support and treatment. Celebrities who use their struggles for good can profoundly impact society. Their willingness to share vulnerabilities and overcome personal obstacles can inspire others to persevere and seek help. Through their advocacy and support for different causes, these individuals contribute to raising awareness, funds, and support networks, making a positive difference in the lives of many. Whether it is through creating foundations, participating in public campaigns, or using their influence to promote dialogue and understanding, celebrities who leverage their struggles for the greater good have the potential to reach a wide audience and spark meaningful change. It is essential to acknowledge and appreciate the efforts of both unsung heroes and well-known figures in using their struggles to make a positive impact on the lives of others. Their combined efforts contribute to a more compassionate and supportive society, creating a ripple effect of inspiration and healing.

Like John, a notable example of an athlete who transformed their pain into a force for good is Michael Phelps, the most decorated Olympian in history. Phelps faced various personal struggles throughout his swimming career, including depression, anxiety, and substance abuse. After the 2012 Olympics, Phelps experienced a period of intense self-reflection and realized that he needed to address his mental health issues. He sought help, engaged in therapy, and made significant lifestyle changes to prioritize his well-being. Following his retirement from competitive swimming after the 2016 Olympics, Phelps became an advocate for mental health awareness. He openly shared his battles with depression and anxiety, breaking down stigmas surrounding mental health in the sports world. Phelps partnered with the Child Mind Institute and launched the Michael Phelps Foundation to promote mental health education and support those in need. Phelps has used his platform and firsthand experiences to inspire and support others facing similar challenges. His advocacy work has encouraged athletes and individuals worldwide to prioritize their mental health, seek help when needed, and break the silence surrounding mental health issues. Phelps' journey demonstrates that even highly accomplished athletes can struggle with their mental well-being. By speaking out and using his influence, he has helped reduce mental health stigma and created a supportive space for others to seek help and find hope. Phelps' dedication to raising awareness and supporting mental health initiatives displays the power of transforming personal pain into a force for good, enabling him to make a lasting impact beyond his sporting achievements.

Resilience and success go hand in hand, as resilient individuals possess qualities and skills contributing to achievement. They exhibit determination, adaptability, and a positive mindset, enabling them to bounce back from failure, setbacks, and obstacles. Cultivating a resilient mindset sets the foundation for long-term success and fulfillment, equipping individuals to navigate challenges, seize opportunities, and persevere on their chosen paths. The power of resilience is undeniable. By understanding resilience at its core, exploring its science, and nurturing resilience in various aspects of our lives, we unlock an inner strength that enables us to navigate life's challenges with grace and fortitude. Resilience empowers us to embrace adversity as an opportunity for growth, bounce back from setbacks, and build fulfilling relationships and careers. The study of resilience has revealed fascinating insights into the psychological and neurological mechanisms behind this remarkable trait. Researchers have discovered that resilience is not only a product of our genetics but also shaped by our environment and individual experiences. They have explored the concept of post-traumatic growth, which shows that individuals can experience positive transformations and personal growth after adversity.

Neuroscience has brought to light fascinating insights into the impact of stress on our brain's structure and function, illuminating the remarkable plasticity of our minds. Research in neuroplasticity has revealed that the brain can adapt, reorganize, and even regenerate itself in response to various experiences and environmental factors, including stress. When we encounter stressful situations, our brain undergoes intricate changes in its neural connections. The stress response triggers the release of hormones, such as cortisol, which can have short-term and long-term effects on our brain's structure and function. In the short term, stress hormones prepare our body to respond to the threat, sharpening our focus and senses.

However, when stress becomes chronic or overwhelming, it can harm our well-being and cognitive abilities. Chronic stress can lead to structural changes in the brain, particularly in regions like the hippocampus, prefrontal cortex, and amygdala. The hippocampus, responsible for memory and learning, can shrink under chronic stress, affecting our ability to retain information and form new memories. The prefrontal cortex, involved in decision-making, impulse control, and emotional regulation, can also be impacted, potentially leading to difficulties in these areas. Additionally, the amygdala, which plays a vital role in processing emotions and fear responses, can become overactive, leading to heightened anxiety and emotional reactivity. However, the fascinating aspect of neuroplasticity is that these changes are not permanent. With intentional efforts and practice, we can positively influence the plasticity of our brains. Engaging in stress-reducing activities, such as mindfulness meditation, exercise, and social support, can help reverse the negative impact of chronic stress on our brains. These practices have been shown to promote the growth of new neurons, increase the density of connections between brain cells, and enhance the brain's overall functioning. The plasticity of our minds means we can rewire and reshape our brains throughout our lives. By actively engaging in stress management techniques, practicing self-care, and adopting healthy coping mechanisms, we can strengthen the resilience of our brains and enhance our ability to adapt to stress. This knowledge underscores the importance of actively nurturing our mental and emotional well-being, as it directly influences the structure and function of our brains.

Neuroscience has provided valuable insights into the impact of stress on our brain's structure and function. The field of neuroplasticity has demonstrated the incredible ability of our brains to adapt and change in response to experiences, including stress. By understanding the plasticity of our minds, we can harness this knowledge to actively cultivate resilience, promote well-being, and mitigate the negative effects of chronic stress. The power to shape our brains and enhance our mental and emotional stability lies within our hands, offering us hope and possibilities for growth and transformation. Though neuroscience provides valuable insights into the impact of stress on our brain's structure and function, the ultimate renewal of our minds comes through the transformative power of reading scripture. While neuroscience helps us understand our brain's physiological and psychological aspects, scripture holds a unique and profound wisdom beyond science. Scripture, particularly the Bible, offers timeless truths, teachings, and narratives that speak directly to the human condition. It provides guidance, comfort, and a sense of purpose that surpasses the limitations of scientific knowledge. The words within scripture carry a divine authority and offer a spiritual lens through which we can view our experiences, struggles, and growth. We engage with hope, resilience, and transformation narratives when we immerse ourselves in scripture reading. We encounter stories of individuals who faced immense challenges and found strength and wisdom through faith. Through their experiences, we gain insight into the power of God's grace, mercy, and love. Scripture encourages us to renew our minds and align our thoughts with God's truth, guiding us toward a life of purpose, peace, and joy. Reading scripture allows us to connect with a higher power and seek divine wisdom beyond our human understanding. It invites us into a relationship with God, providing us with a source of comfort, guidance, and transformation. The words within scripture can penetrate our hearts, challenge our perspectives, and inspire us to live in alignment with our identity as children of God. Scripture offers a framework for ethical and moral living. It provides principles and teachings that shape our values, relationships, and decisions. Reading scripture gives us insight into how to navigate the complexities of life, make choices that honor God and others, and find healing and restoration in times of brokenness. As we engage with scripture, we invite God's wisdom and truth to renew our minds, shaping us into individuals who embody resilience, love, and the fullness of life.

Selah

How can I transform my pain into purpose?

Take a moment to reflect on your own experiences of pain and hardship. Consider the challenges you have faced and the emotions they have stirred within you. Now, shift your perspective and explore how to use these experiences to fuel a greater sense of purpose in your life.

Ask yourself: How can I harness the lessons from my pain and transform them into a driving force for meaningful change and growth? What passions, talents, or strengths can I cultivate through my pain to positively impact myself and others? How can I contribute to the healing and well-being of others facing similar struggles?

In this reflection, identify the unseen benefits amidst the pain, the seeds of resilience and wisdom that have emerged from your hardships. Consider how your experiences have shaped your values, priorities, and sense of empathy. How can you use these insights to create a purpose aligned with your core values and desires?

Furthermore, reflect on the steps you can take to embrace your pain and allow it to drive you toward a greater purpose. How can you channel your emotions, experiences, and newfound wisdom into actions that bring about positive change? How can you leverage your pain to catalyze personal growth, healing, and transformation?

Remember, turning pain into purpose is deeply personal and unique to everyone. It requires introspection, self-compassion, and a willingness to confront the difficult aspects of your journey. Embrace this reflective question as an opportunity to unearth the transformative power within your pain and discover how it can shape your purpose, allowing you to find greater meaning, fulfillment, and impact in your life.

THIS IS YOUR PERSONAL SPACE

WRITE HOW YOU WILL

REFRESH, ESCAPE, SOOTHE, TRANQUILIZE

Let Yourself Rest

DATE:

I WILL REST TODAY BY...

CHAPTER 7

Pain to Purpose and Beyond

TRANSITIONING FROM PAIN to purpose is a transformative journey that can bring profound meaning and fulfillment. As we navigate the challenges and hardships that life presents us, we can harness the lessons learned from our pain and forge a path toward purpose. However, we may contemplate what comes next once we have discovered our goal. We often experience profound clarity and direction when transitioning from pain to purpose. Our purpose gives us a sense of meaning, propelling us forward and guiding our choices. It becomes a driving force that motivates us to make a positive impact, contribute to the world, and live in alignment with our values. Purpose becomes the compass that helps us navigate the complexities of life.

But what lies beyond purpose? After we have found our calling and aligned our lives with it, we may find ourselves seeking further growth and expansion. We may realize that purpose is not a destination but an ongoing journey of self-discovery and evolution. Beyond purpose lies the realm of possibility and potential. It is a space where we continue to explore and refine our goals, deepening our understanding of ourselves and our impact on the world. It is a freedom where we embrace lifelong learning, open ourselves to new experiences, and remain flexible to the possibilities that unfold before us. We discover that purpose is not a static concept but a fluid and dynamic force that evolves with us. Our goal may expand, taking on new dimensions and challenging us to reach new heights. We leverage our goals and collective strengths to inspire, uplift, and empower those around us. Through our purpose, we can foster meaningful connections, create positive change, and contribute to the greater good. As we reflect on transitioning from pain to purpose and beyond, we are reminded that our journey is a continuous unfolding of self-discovery, growth, and impact. It encourages us to remain open to new possibilities, embrace change and development, and continuously seek alignment with our authentic selves. In this ongoing journey, we may find that purpose leads us to new goals, opening doors we never anticipated.

We were all created with a purpose, and whether grand or small, our unique contributions will always be effective in the intricate fabric of life. "Driven Purpose Life" by Rick Warren is a profound and inspiring book that guides readers toward discovering and living a purpose-driven life. Warren shares his insights and wisdom on how to find meaning and fulfillment by aligning one's life with God's purpose. The book emphasizes the importance of understanding that God uniquely designed us with a specific goal. Warren encourages readers to seek God's guidance and wisdom in discovering their purpose and trust in His divine plan. Warren addresses various aspects of life through practical advice and relatable anecdotes, including relationships, work, and personal growth. He guides how to integrate faith into all areas of life, emphasizing the significance of living with integrity and positively impacting the world. The book also explores the power of prayer, the importance of building strong and meaningful relationships, and the value of using one's gifts and talents to serve others. Warren emphasizes the role of selflessness, gratitude, and perseverance in living a purpose-driven life. Throughout the book, he offers biblical teachings and insights that inspire readers to embrace their God-given purpose and live with intentionality. He emphasizes the transformative power of aligning one's life with God's purpose, leading to a life filled with joy, meaning, and deep fulfillment. Through practical advice, biblical teachings, and personal anecdotes, Rick Warren empowers readers to discover their unique purpose, align their lives with God's plan, and find true fulfillment in serving others and living in faith. The book is a powerful resource for those seeking to deepen their understanding of the purpose and live a life that truly matters. Imagine how we can impact the world by turning our pain into purpose.

While Mordecai Ham may not be widely known by the public today, one individual he impacted during his evangelistic campaigns became quite famous. That individual was Billy Graham, who became one of the most influential Christian evangelists of his time and had a global impact through his preaching and ministry. Mordecai Ham's influence on Billy Graham's spiritual journey highlights the profound effect that one person can have on the life of another, even if they may not achieve widespread recognition. As a traveling evangelist, Mordecai conducted revival meetings and crusades across different cities and towns. Through his powerful and impactful preaching, Ham aimed to bring people to a deep understanding of sin, the need for repentance, and the transformative power of faith in Jesus Christ. His enthusiastic delivery and unwavering commitment to the truth inspired countless individuals to commit to Christ and experience spiritual transformation. Ham dedicated himself to preaching the Gospel, calling people to turn away from sin, embrace God's forgiveness, and live a life of faith and obedience. By faithfully conducting his ministry, Mordecai Ham fulfilled his purpose of sharing the message of salvation, leading people to Christ, and nurturing their spiritual growth. His tireless efforts, powerful sermons, and commitment to living out his faith had a lasting impact on the lives of those who heard him speak. Mordecai Ham's purpose extended beyond the revival meetings and crusading he conducted. He left a legacy of inspiring and equipping others to continue spreading the Gospel. Many individuals influenced by his ministry became pastors, evangelists, and leaders, continuing to share the message of salvation and impact lives for generations to come.

Mordecai Ham played a significant role in guiding Billy Graham's faith journey. In 1934, when Billy Graham was just 15 years old, he attended a series of revival meetings led by Ham in Charlotte, North Carolina. During one of those meetings, Graham experienced a spiritual awakening and felt a deep conviction in his heart. He realized the need for a personal relationship with God and committed his life to Christ. During this time, he made a public profession of faith and began his journey as a follower of Jesus. The impact of Mordecai Ham's evangelistic preaching on Graham was profound. Ham's sermons challenged Graham to consider the reality of sin, the need for salvation, and the Gospel's transformative power. His words ignited a passion within Graham to share the message of God's love and forgiveness with others. Following his conversion, Billy Graham continued to pursue his education, eventually attending Wheaton College, where he deepened his knowledge of the Bible and grew in his faith. Over time, Graham's ministry as an evangelist began to take shape, and he became known for his powerful preaching, integrity, and commitment to spreading the Gospel worldwide. While Mordecai Ham is known for his impactful ministry and influential preaching, he, like many others, experienced his share of struggles and sufferings throughout his life. These personal challenges shaped his character and deepened his understanding of human suffering and the redemptive power of God's love. One significant hardship in Ham's life was losing his first wife, Mabel Hamilton. Her passing left him grief-stricken and grappling with the pain of losing a loved one. The experience of navigating through this sorrowful period allowed Ham to empathize with those who had endured similar losses and gave him a deeper understanding of the human experience of suffering. Additionally, Mordecai Ham faced opposition and criticism for his uncompromising message of repentance and salvation. His bold stance on moral issues and unwavering commitment to sharing the Gospel often drew praise and condemnation from various quarters. These challenges tested his resolve and required him to persevere amidst adversity. Moreover, as a traveling evangelist, Ham encountered the daily trials and tribulations associated with a nomadic lifestyle. The physical demands, financial uncertainties, and constant upheaval can take a toll on anyone. Still, Ham's faith in God's provision and his conviction in the importance of his ministry kept him steadfast despite these challenges. Through his own experiences of struggle and suffering, Mordecai Ham developed a profound compassion for others facing similar difficulties. He connected with individuals in their pain, offering them hope and encouragement through the message of God's love and redemption. His journey of overcoming hardship was a powerful testimony of God's faithfulness and the transformative power of faith.

It is important to recognize that while Mordecai Ham's struggles and sufferings were part of his life, they did not define him. Rather, he used these experiences to deepen his empathy, strengthen his character, and fuel his passion for sharing the message of salvation. His ability to transcend his difficulties and focus on God's redemptive work is a testament to his resilience and unwavering commitment to his purpose. Personal struggles and sufferings marked Mordecai Ham's life he encountered. These challenges shaped him, deepened his empathy, and enhanced his ability to connect with others. Through his own experiences, he offered hope, encouragement, and the transformative message of God's love to those facing trials and tribulations. His life serves as a reminder that even amid struggles, God's grace can sustain and empower individuals to fulfill their purpose and impact the lives of others.

Billy Graham shared the story of his conversion experience throughout his life and credited Mordecai Ham's influence as a key turning point in his spiritual journey. The encounter with Ham led Graham to faith and shaped his calling to proclaim the message of salvation to millions of people around the globe. Billy Graham's story is a testament to the profound impact that individuals can have on shaping the faith of others. Graham's life was transformed through the guidance of Mordecai Ham and his encounter with God. He became one of the most influential Christian evangelists of the 20th century, touching the lives of countless individuals with the message of hope, redemption, and God's love. Billy Graham's impact extended beyond his ministry and touched the lives of numerous individuals, including several presidents of the United States. Throughout his career, Graham served as an advisor and spiritual counselor to multiple presidents, regardless of their political affiliations.

Graham had personal relationships and guided presidents such as Harry S. Truman, Dwight D. Eisenhower, Lyndon B. Johnson, Richard Nixon, Ronald Reagan, and many others. He prayed with them, offered spiritual support, and often participated in national prayer services and events at the invitation of the presidents. His influence went beyond personal relationships. Graham conducted numerous evangelistic crusades, televised sermons, and authored books that reached millions worldwide. His messages of faith, hope, and redemption resonated with diverse audiences, transcending political boundaries. Graham's impact on presidents and their leadership was significant, as his counsel often influenced their decisions, moral compass, and understanding of religious matters. His emphasis on integrity, unity, and the importance of faith played a role in shaping the lives and leadership styles of those he encountered. The relationship between Graham and the presidents of the United States demonstrates how the impact of an individual can extend far beyond their immediate sphere of influence. Graham's work exemplifies the profound effect one person can have on the lives of many, including those in positions of power and authority. Mordecai Ham's impact on Billy Graham's life, which eventually led to Graham's global influence, exemplifies how one person's contribution, even if not widely recognized, can have a profound ripple effect. It highlights the interconnectedness of individuals and the idea that each person's purpose, whether seen or unseen, contributes to the bigger picture of life. Each person, including you, my dear reader, has a unique sense, and not all roles require being at the forefront of seeking widespread recognition. Just as the trunk provides essential support for the tree's growth and allows its vibrant foliage to flourish, individuals who work behind the scenes or provide support play a crucial role in enabling others to shine. The analogy serves as a reminder that every part, whether in the spotlight or behind the scenes, is essential for society's collective growth and beauty. Regardless of the scale or recognition, each person's unique purpose and contribution holds intrinsic value in the grand scheme. It is through combined efforts and diverse roles that the world can experience its full potential and beauty.

Selah

Here is a reflective exercise to explore the theme of turning pain into purpose and going beyond:

1. Recall a momentous experience or period of pain or adversity. It could be a personal struggle, a challenging situation, or a painful event. Take some time to reflect on the emotions, lessons, and impact it had on you.

2. Ask yourself: What did I learn from this experience? How did it shape me as a person? Did it ignite any desire or passion within me?

3. Consider how you have transformed that pain into purpose. Have you used your experience to help others, create positive change, or develop a greater understanding of yourself and the world?

4. Reflect on the journey beyond pain and purpose. Have there been moments when you realized the impact of your actions or the influence you have had? How have you grown and evolved beyond the initial pain?

5. Write your thoughts, insights, and reflections in your notebook or journal. Take the time to express your feelings and articulate any emerging realizations.

6. Explore how you can continue to go beyond your initial purpose. Are there new ways you can utilize your experiences and strengths to make an even greater impact? Are there areas where you can further grow and develop?

7. Consider the lessons and wisdom you have gained from this exercise. How can you apply these insights to your life moving forward? Can you make specific actions or changes to align with your purpose and continue evolving?

8. Close the exercise by expressing gratitude for the journey, the pain that shaped you, the purpose you have found, and the potential for growth and impact that lies ahead.

Remember, this reflective exercise is a personal exploration. Take your time, be honest, and allow the insights to unfold naturally. Embrace the process of turning pain into purpose and the limitless potential within you.

THIS IS YOUR PERSONAL SPACE

WRITE HOW YOU WILL

REFRESH, ESCAPE, SOOTHE, TRANQUILIZE

LET. yourself -REST-

DATE:

I WILL REST TODAY BY...

CHAPTER 8

The Art of
Letting Go

"I HAVE BEEN seeking rest since I published "The Beginning Starts at the End" in 2017. Seeking rest from past struggles is a courageous and transformative journey that allows us to break free from the chains of our past and embrace a life of freedom, peace, and wholeness. Reflecting on my pursuit of rest from past struggles, I am reminded of the steps and mindset that have helped me along the way.

Firstly, I acknowledge the power of self-compassion. I am human and have made mistakes or faced challenges that have impacted me deeply. By extending grace and understanding to myself, I can release the burden of self-blame and embrace a mindset of healing and growth.

Next, I actively engage in the process of self-reflection. I courageously confront the pain and discomfort of my past struggles, allowing myself to process the associated emotions. Through journaling, therapy, or conversations with trusted individuals, I explore the roots of my works, seeking understanding and clarity.

I forgive others and myself. I recognize that holding onto resentment and anger only hinders my ability to find rest and move forward. By choosing to ignore, I release the weight of anger and open myself to the healing power of reconciliation and inner peace. In addition to God helping me overcome anger, I read a life-changing book.

"Good and Angry: Letting Go of Anger, Irritation, Complaining, and Bitterness" by David Powlison is a transformative book that explores the complex emotions of anger and provides practical guidance for navigating and managing them healthily and constructively. In this book, Powlison dives deep into the roots of anger, acknowledging its potential for both harm and good. He highlights how anger can stem from various sources, such as injustice, personal offense, frustration, or unmet desires. Through real-life stories, biblical wisdom, and practical insights, Powlison offers readers a fresh perspective on anger and presents a pathway toward freedom and healing. Powlison emphasizes the importance of understanding the underlying causes of anger and offers practical strategies for addressing and transforming it. He guides readers through examining their hearts, exploring their beliefs, and identifying the unhelpful patterns and habits contributing to unhealthy anger. Moreover, "Good and Angry" delves into the destructive manifestations of anger, such as bitterness, complaining, and irritability. Powlison provides biblical wisdom and practical tools to break free from these negative patterns and develop healthier responses to anger. Throughout the book, Powlison highlights the role of God's grace and the gospel's transformative power in the context of anger. He encourages readers to seek God's perspective, extend forgiveness, and pursue reconciliation in their relationships. "Good and Angry" offers a comprehensive approach to understanding and transforming anger. It equips readers with practical tools, biblical principles, and real-life examples to navigate the complexities of anger and find freedom from its destructive grip. It is a valuable resource for anyone seeking to cultivate healthy and God-honoring responses to anger, leading to greater peace, restoration, and wholeness.

Additionally, I actively seek support from a community of loved ones, mentors, or professionals who can provide guidance, empathy, and encouragement. Sharing my struggles and vulnerabilities with trusted individuals lightens the burden and helps me gain valuable insights and perspectives, contributing to my healing journey. As I navigate the path to rest, I make intentional choices to nurture my mental, emotional, and physical well-being. I prioritize self-care activities that bring me joy, whether engaging in hobbies, practicing mindfulness, pursuing healthy relationships, or caring for my body through exercise and nourishing food. These practices replenish my energy and improve my overall sense of rest and rejuvenation.

Most importantly, I lean on my faith and trust in God. I find solace and strength in my spiritual connection, seeking guidance, comfort, and healing through prayer, meditation, and studying scripture. Through my faith, I find rest in knowing that I am not alone on this journey and that divine love and grace are always available to support me. I am committed to living a life of freedom, joy, and purpose, and I am determined to find rest as I continue to embrace healing, self-discovery, and the pursuit of my fullest potential.

Two powerful books that have helped me find true rest in Jesus Christ - "Streams in the Desert" is a devotional book that offers spiritual nourishment and encouragement for weary souls. Its timeless messages and reflections can provide rest in several ways, even in our modern-day lives. "Streams in the Desert" offers a respite from the chaos and busyness of life. Its poetic and contemplative nature invites readers to pause, reflect, and find solace in the words of wisdom and encouragement in its pages. By taking moments to engage with the book's profound insights, we can experience a sense of calm and rest amid the demands and distractions of our daily routines. It brings comfort and encouragement during times of struggle and adversity. The book is filled with anecdotes, stories, and scriptural passages that speak to the reality of pain, hardship, and uncertainty in life. These pages remind us of God's faithfulness, provision, and grace. This reassurance can bring rest to our weary hearts as we navigate the challenges and trials that come our way. It offers a renewed perspective on our circumstances. It prompts us to shift our focus from the temporary and transient to the eternal and unchanging. The book invites us to trust God's sovereignty, find strength in His promises, and discover meaning and purpose amid difficulties. This shift in perspective can bring rest to our minds and hearts as we anchor ourselves in the unshakable truth of God's love and faithfulness. Moreover, "Streams in the Desert" fosters a deeper connection with God. Its daily readings and reflections encourage us to seek intimate communion with our Heavenly Father. Through its pages, we are reminded to turn to God in prayer, to listen for His voice, and to trust in His guidance. This invitation to draw near God and experience His presence can bring rest to our souls as we find comfort and strength in our relationship with Him. "Streams in the Desert" offers us rest by providing a source of spiritual nourishment, comfort, and guidance. It reminds us of God's unfailing love, sustaining grace, and presence with us in every season of life. By engaging with the book's timeless wisdom and insights, we can find rest for our weary souls and be refreshed in our faith journey.

The second and favored book is "The Imitation of Christ, "by Thomas Kempis.

In my journey, this book has played a significant role in helping me find rest in Christ alone. At its core, "The Imitation of Christ" calls us to cultivate a deep and intimate relationship with Jesus, to follow His example, and to align our lives with His teachings. Through its powerful insights and reflections, the book has guided me to seek rest not in the fleeting comforts of the world but in Christ's abiding presence and love. One of the key lessons I have learned from "The Imitation of Christ" is the importance of surrendering my desires and ambitions to God's will. It has taught me that true rest is found when I let go of my agenda and submit to God's perfect plan for my life. I have discovered a deep sense of peace and fulfillment that transcends worldly pursuits by imitating Christ's humility, obedience, and selflessness. "The Imitation of Christ" has also helped me to prioritize the eternal over the temporal. It reminds me that the pursuits of this world, such as wealth, success, or recognition, can never truly satisfy the longing of my soul. Instead, it directs me to seek God's kingdom and righteousness. This shift in perspective has allowed me to find rest from the restlessness that comes from chasing after empty pursuits. Furthermore, the book emphasizes the importance of prayer and contemplation in finding rest in Christ. It encourages me to carve out intentional moments of silence and solitude, commune with God, and listen to His gentle whispers. Through these moments of stillness, I have experienced the peace that surpasses understanding and a deep sense of connection with my Creator. "The Imitation of Christ" has also challenged me to examine my heart and confront areas of spiritual pride, self-righteousness, and selfishness. It calls me to embrace a life of humility, love, and service, mirroring the example of Christ. In doing so, I have found rest from the burdensome weight of self-centered living and discovered the joy of selfless giving and sacrificial love.

"The Imitation of Christ" has been a transformative companion on my spiritual journey, guiding me toward a deeper union with Christ and helping me find rest in Him alone. Its timeless wisdom reminded me that true rest is found in imitating Christ, surrendering to His will, prioritizing the eternal, cultivating a life of prayer and contemplation, and embracing humility and selfless love. It has been a source of inspiration, guidance, and solace, leading me to find rest in the arms of my Savior, who offers rest to all who come to Him with open hearts.

Join me on this transformative journey as we discover the rest we long for. In a world filled with busyness, distractions, and constant demands, losing sight of what truly brings rest to our weary souls is easy. Let us cast aside our burdens, worries, and anxieties and pursue what belongs to us.

My dear reader, I invite you to embark on this journey of finding rest. We will discover a rest that transcends circumstances, a rest that renews our spirits, and a rest that restores our souls. Let us walk this path together.

THIS IS YOUR PERSONAL SPACE

WRITE HOW YOU WILL

REFRESH, ESCAPE, SOOTHE, TRANQUILIZE

DATE:

I WILL REST TODAY BY...

CHAPTER 9

Come and Find Rest

FOR SOMEONE WHO does not follow Christ or hold Christian beliefs, the invitation to find rest in Christ may have a different meaning or significance. However, stay with me. Concluding the book without sharing would not align with my newfound understanding and the growth I have experienced. Reflecting upon my past, I recognize the mistakes I made in presuming ownership of Christianity, which regrettably led me down a path of judgment, self-righteousness, and condemnation toward those with differing beliefs. To do justice to the evolution of my perspective and to ensure an authentic expression of love and compassion, I must approach the conclusion of this book with a different message. It is imperative to embrace inclusivity, empathy, and an unwavering commitment to fostering a spirit of understanding and acceptance among all individuals, regardless of their faith or worldview. Rather than perpetuating divisiveness, I desire to promote unity, encouraging diversity of human beliefs and experiences. Hopefully, we all embark on a collective journey towards empathy, where genuine connections are forged, and mutual respect is cherished. By recognizing the transformative power of love, compassion, and the profound value inherent in every human being, we can foster an environment that nurtures harmony, understanding, and deep personal growth. Let this book catalyze introspection, urging readers to examine their preconceptions, biases, and judgments. Together, let us strive to foster a more open-hearted approach, recognizing that embracing diverse perspectives enriches our understanding of the world and promotes a more harmonious coexistence. May the concluding chapters resonate with the universal values that transcend religious boundaries, reminding us of every individual's intrinsic worth and dignity. In doing so, we share our journey toward a future illuminated by acceptance.

In the vast expanse of my expedition, I have traversed the labyrinthine depths of seeking rest, yearning for respite amidst the trials and tribulations of existence. My efforts were fruitless as I sought refuge in the precarious realms of self-reliance, human relationships, fleeting circumstances, meritorious achievements, and the ceaseless pursuit of external validation. These ephemeral realms proved to be wellsprings of depletion, leaving me more bereft and forlorn than ever before. Yet, within the recesses of my soul, a yearning persisted, urging me to plunge further into the profound depths of existence. I searched in quiet introspection and tranquil stillness, delving into the hushed realms of contemplation. In the serene embrace of silence, I encountered the glorious presence of Christ, excelling the constricting bounds of religious fears and dogmas and emerging as the embodiment of boundless love itself. Christ's love surpasses human understanding and is the quintessence of divine affection and compassion. It is a love that exceeds all boundaries, unshackling hearts and liberating souls from the constraints of judgment and fear. Christ is not the source of fear or apprehension for most individuals. Rather, the religious institutions and practices associated with Christianity may sometimes evoke reservations in people. Christ personifies love, compassion, and the example of divine grace. His teachings emphasize acceptance, forgiveness, and unconditional love. In the pursuit of truth and meaning, it is crucial to discern between the essence of Christ's teachings and the interpretations and practices of religious institutions. By recognizing the fundamental messages of love, compassion, and understanding that Christ represents, we can grasp a broader perspective and appreciate the values that unite humanity. As hard as it may seem, seek the essence of His teachings, overcome religious limitations, and experience the love that can illuminate life and bring about reflective and spiritual growth. My search for rest, once futile, was sublimely fulfilled in the stillness, silence, and solitude. In such a presence, I discovered a haven of serenity, a sanctuary where weariness dissipated and burdens were lifted. No longer bound by the shackles of self-reliance, I found rejuvenation in surrendering to the peace that defines Christ. Let my tale be a testament to such transformation, an invitation to all who seek rest. Beyond the ephemeral facades of transient worldly pursuits lies a realm where love reigns supreme, beckoning us to incorporate its profound embrace. In this sacred space, we discover the resplendence of 1 Corinthians 13, irradiating our path toward reconciliation with Christ. May this revelation be a guiding light, inspiring fellow sojourners to embark upon their quest for rest and igniting a flame of curiosity that overtakes all barriers.

Rest from Denial

We spend considerable time denying the existence of Christ rather than actively pursuing a personal understanding or connection with

Him. This stems from several reasons, including differing beliefs, skepticism, or a lack of exposure to the teachings and experiences associated with Christ. However, it is essential to recognize that pursuing a personal understanding of Christ is an individual journey. It requires an open mind, curiosity, and a willingness to explore one's spirituality and beliefs. Rather than focusing on denial or negation, investing time and energy in seeking personal meaning and connection can be more fruitful. By engaging in thoughtful inquiry, exploring the teachings attributed to Christ, and reflecting on one's own experiences and beliefs, individuals can embark on a journey of personal discovery and connection with the principles that Christ represents. This pursuit is a deeply personal and subjective process that can lead to a greater understanding of oneself, the world, and one's spiritual path. Instead of engaging in debates or resistance, consider focusing on self-reflection, introspection, and fostering an open heart and mind. Allow the possibility of a personal connection to unfold naturally, without the pressure of external expectations or influences.

"Seeking Allah, Finding Christ" is a book by Nabeel Qureshi, a convert to Christianity. The book chronicles Qureshi's spiritual exploration journey and eventual conversion to Christianity. In his book, Qureshi shares his experiences growing up in a devout Muslim family, his encounters with Christians, his study of Islam and Christianity, and his internal struggles as he wrestled with questions of faith and truth. Throughout the book, Qureshi explores the teachings and claims of Islam and Christianity, delving into theological and historical examinations of both religions. He candidly shares the challenges he encountered, the doubts he grappled with, and the deep personal transformation he experienced in his journey toward embracing Christ. Qureshi's book serves as a testimony to the profound impact spiritual exploration and encountering different beliefs can have on an individual's faith journey. It offers insights into the complex interplay of individual experiences, intellectual examination, and the heart's inner workings in pursuing truth and meaning. "Seeking Allah, Finding Christ" provides a unique perspective on the intersections between Islam and Christianity and allows readers to gain insight into the deeply personal and transformative journey.

"The Case for Christ" is a book by a former atheist and investigative journalist, Lee Strobel. In his book, Strobel sets out on a mission to disprove the claims of Christianity by examining the historical evidence surrounding the life, death, and resurrection of Jesus Christ. As an avowed skeptic, Strobel meticulously investigates various aspects of the Christian faith, including the Gospels' reliability, the evidence for Jesus' divinity, and the credibility of eyewitness accounts. Throughout his research, he engages with scholars, theologians, and experts in their respective fields, seeking answers to his questions and doubts. However, during his investigation, Strobel encounters compelling evidence and persuasive arguments that challenge his initial skepticism. He grapples with the weight of historical and eyewitness testimony, archaeological discoveries, and expert analysis, leading him to a profound personal transformation. "The Case for Christ" presents Strobel's journey from skepticism to faith, highlighting the impact of his investigation on his own beliefs and worldview. The book serves as a testament to the power of intellectual inquiry and the exploration of evidence, as Strobel finds himself confronted with the compelling case for the historical reality and significance of Jesus Christ. While initially attempting to disprove Christ, Strobel discovers a faith he had not anticipated. His journey illustrates the transformative power of honest inquiry, critical examination, and a willingness to follow the evidence wherever it leads. "The Case for Christ" has become influential in apologetics and has resonated with many readers seeking answers to intellectual objections regarding Christianity. It offers a unique perspective on the personal journey of a skeptic who, through a rigorous investigation, finds compelling reasons to embrace the claims of Christ.

I present this notion not to sway or compel but to illuminate a sentiment close to my heart. When I uncover innovative paths and discover treatments that nurture wellness, facilitate success, or herald positive transformations, I have an innate desire to share these findings with others. Why, may you wonder? The answer resides in the profound enrichment that such knowledge has bestowed upon me. In pursuing personal growth and well-being, stumbling upon novel approaches or therapies is akin to unearthing precious gems amidst the vast expanse of existence. The discovery of these transformative measures evokes a deep sense of gratitude and an impulse to extend the benefits to fellow seekers of truth and fulfillment. My intention is not to impose or proselytize but rather to foster a spirit of collective upliftment. By sharing the insights and experiences that have positively impacted my journey, I aim to create a ripple effect of sharing, fostering an environment where others may also embrace the gifts of well-being, success, and positivity. In recognizing the inherent value of disseminating knowledge that has enriched my life, I offer a gesture of benevolence, paving the way for others to embark upon their transformative quests. By sharing, I aspire to cultivate a sense of unity, a bond forged through exchanging wisdom, and a mutual commitment to fulfillment. Through the willingness to share our discoveries, we coalesce into a supportive community united in our pursuit of wellness, success, and realizing our fullest potential. Should these insights resonate with your being, let them serve as incentives for personal exploration. In this endeavor, let us contribute to humanity's enlightenment and collective betterment.

Rest from Confusion

When we turn to Christ, we discover a refuge—a place of rest where our souls can find renewal and restoration. We have a spiritual void or longing that can only be fulfilled by having a relationship with Christ or finding spiritual rest in Him. The idea is that the spirit, or soul, finds its ultimate purpose, meaning, and fulfillment in connection with Jesus Christ. We possess a non-material or immaterial essence beyond the physical body and mind. Unfortunately, we struggle to find our way to Jesus or believe we are not good enough to approach Him due to perceived limitations or exclusions imposed by human rules or interpretations. Jesus is often portrayed as a figure who welcomes all who seek Him, regardless of their background or past. It is important to approach religious beliefs and interpretations with an open mind and to remember that Jesus' message is one of inclusivity. It is possible that the term "Christianity" or the various denominational divisions within Christianity can lead to limitations or confinements in how people perceive and approach Jesus. These divisions can sometimes create barriers or exclusions, causing individuals to feel disconnected or unworthy of approaching Jesus. However, it is important to remember that Jesus does not label us like we do. His message was for everyone, regardless of religious affiliations or denominational boundaries. The word "Christian" originated in the early days of the

Christian faith and was first used in Antioch to describe the disciples of Jesus Christ. Christianity, at its core, was never meant to exclude people. The inclusive nature of Christianity can be seen in various aspects of Jesus' ministry. He engaged with people from diverse social classes, including tax collectors, sinners, Samaritans, and Gentiles, breaking his time's social and cultural barriers. His message of salvation and redemption was intended for all humanity, and his ultimate sacrifice on the cross was for the salvation of everyone who believed in Him. Throughout history, human interpretations and practices within Christianity have sometimes deviated from this inclusive vision. Divisions, conflicts, and exclusions have arisen, often driven by differences in beliefs, doctrines, or cultural factors. These human shortcomings and misinterpretations have led to instances where people have been excluded or marginalized in the name of Christianity. When understood and practiced in line with its foundational principles of inclusivity and acceptance, Christianity can embrace all people and foster a sense of unity and community.

People can find rest from confusing God with Christians. One way to find it is to dive deeper into the study of Scripture. This deeper knowledge helps us distinguish between the eternal truth of who God is and the imperfect representations we may encounter in the actions or beliefs of Christians. It is also important to remember that humans, including Christians, are on a journey of growth and transformation. We are all works in progress and make mistakes along the way. Recognizing this allows us to extend grace and understanding to ourselves and others, knowing we all need God's mercy and forgiveness. Building relationships with mature and spiritually grounded Christians can be invaluable in finding rest from this confusion. Engaging in discussions, seeking mentorship, and learning from those who have a deeper understanding of God's character can help clarify misunderstandings and provide a more accurate picture of who God truly is. Practicing discernment is another essential aspect. By relying on the guidance of the Holy Spirit, we can navigate the differences between Christians' actions, beliefs, and teachings and the unchanging truth of God's Word. This discernment helps us distinguish between the fallibility of human beings and the infallibility of God's nature and His Word. God's faithfulness is unwavering. He is true to His promises, and His Word stands firm. Despite the inconsistencies we may witness in the actions of Christians, we can rely on the steadfastness of God's character. He will never abandon or forsake us and remains faithful even when others fall short. Giving God a chance means opening our hearts to His presence, seeking Him in prayer, and delving into His Word to discover His truth for ourselves. So, let us not allow the actions or attitudes of Christians to cloud our perception of God. Instead, let us give God a chance to show us who He truly is.

Rest in Silence

Amid a noisy and chaotic world, a sacred universe beckons us—a place of profound rest. We discover a powerful avenue to peace in silence. It offers a respite from the constant stream of thoughts, distractions, and external stimuli that bombard our minds and hearts. It provides an opportunity to quiet the noise within us and attune ourselves to the whispers of our souls. We find a sanctuary where we can replenish our spirits and reconnect with our innermost selves. In silence, we are invited to let go of life's busyness and demands and be present. In this stillness, we can release our burdens, surrender our worries, and find comfort in the knowledge that we are held and supported by something greater than ourselves. Without external noise, we can tune in to the whispers of our hearts and gain clarity about our values, desires, and true priorities in life. We can experience a profound connection with our divine presence in the hushed moments of quiet contemplation. In this stillness, we can listen to our intuition's whispers and our souls' gentle guidance. Finding rest in silence does not require elaborate rituals or specific techniques. It can be simple as setting aside a few moments each day to sit quietly, close our eyes, and be present. It may involve practicing mindfulness, meditation, or engaging in activities that bring us peace and stillness. We can uncover a deep well of peace, healing, and restoration in silence. Create intentional moments of quietude and discover clarity within the depths of silence.

Rest in Solitude

Silence leads to another sacred path, a way of solitude. Solitude allows us to disconnect from the world's noise and find solace in our company. We can retreat into ourselves and reconnect with our deepest thoughts, emotions, and aspirations. We are free to be fully present with ourselves without the pressures of social expectations or the need for constant engagement. In this calmness, we can listen to the whispers of our souls and gain a deeper understanding of who we truly are. Solitude provides us with an opportunity for introspection, self-reflection, and personal growth. As we spend time alone, we can engage in activities that bring us joy, such as reading, writing, or pursuing creative endeavors. We can also engage in practices like meditation or mindfulness, which help us cultivate a sense of inner calm and stillness. Finding rest in isolation does not mean isolating ourselves from others or avoiding meaningful relationships. Instead, it is about intentionally carving out moments of aloneness to nourish our souls and cultivate inner peace. It is about balancing our need for social connection with personal introspection and self-care. In the sanctuary of solitude, we can find respite from the noise and demands of the world.

Rest from Pleasing People

In a world that often places great emphasis on seeking the approval and validation of others, another path leads to deep rest—an invitation to find rest in not pleasing people. This challenges us to break free from the exhausting cycle of trying to meet the expectations and demands of others and, instead, embrace the freedom and peace that comes from living authentically and true to ourselves. Finding this rest begins with recognizing that our worth and value are not dependent on the opinions or acceptance of others. It requires a shift in mindset, where we prioritize our own well-being and inner alignment over the need for external validation. When we release the burden of constantly trying to please others, we create space for self-acceptance. We recognize that it is impossible to meet everyone's expectations, and that is okay. Embracing our imperfections and honoring our unique individuality allows us to enter a place of self-compassion and authenticity. It further involves setting healthy boundaries. It means learning to say no when necessary and recognizing that our time, energy, and resources are valuable and finite. By honoring our needs and limits, we prioritize our well-being and find the rest we deserve. In this journey, we must surround ourselves with a supportive community of individuals who accept and appreciate us for who we are. Establishing relationships that value authenticity and respect our boundaries allows us to find rest in knowing that we are loved and accepted for our true selves. Finding rest in not pleasing people is about reclaiming our power and living in alignment with our values, passions, and purpose. It means honoring our inner compass and making choices that resonate with our hearts, even if they may not please everyone around us. We can experience peace in the freedom of not pleasing people. Let us release the need to seek the approval of others constantly. Let us embrace the beauty of authenticity and find rest in honoring our needs, boundaries, and aspirations.

Rest from Service
(make a note that this is rest, not a call to quit service)

Finding rest in not serving when we are depleted is a crucial act of self-preservation in a realm that often deifies constant productivity. It involves recognizing our limitations and honoring our need for replenishment. Society expects us always to be available, say yes to every request, and constantly give of ourselves. However, true rest comes from understanding that we cannot pour from an empty cup. When we serve others from emptiness, we risk depleting ourselves physically and emotionally. Finding rest in not helping when exhausted requires us to set boundaries and prioritize our well-being. Doing so ensures that we have the energy needed to serve others effectively when in a better state. This practice involves listening to our bodies, minds, and hearts. When we feel physically exhausted, emotionally drained, or mentally overwhelmed, it indicates that we need to pause and prioritize self-care. In these moments of rest, we can replenish our energy, gain clarity, and regain a sense of balance and well-being. It also means letting go of any guilt or societal pressures that may arise. It is essential to understand that taking care of ourselves is not selfish but necessary for our overall health and the quality of the service we provide when we are in a better state. By doing so, we set an example for others to do the same. We show that finding a healthy balance between serving others and caring for ourselves is possible. It reminds us that our well-being is important and that by caring for ourselves, we can better show up for others when we can truly serve from a place of authenticity, compassion, and abundance.

"Having a Mary Heart in a Martha World" by Joanna Weaver is a transformative book that explores the timeless story of Mary and Martha from the Bible and offers insights on building a deep and intimate relationship with God amid a busy and demanding world. Weaver delves into the familiar biblical narrative of Mary and Martha, two sisters with contrasting approaches to their time with Jesus. Martha is known for her busyness and preoccupation with serving, while Mary chooses to sit at Jesus' feet, listening and learning from Him. Through this story, Weaver highlights the tension many faces in prioritizing a life of devotion and intimacy with God amidst the distractions and pressures of everyday life. The book offers practical guidance on developing a "Mary heart" in a "Martha world," accentuating the importance of nurturing a heart primarily seeking to know and love God. Weaver encourages readers to slow down, silence the noise, and create space for God in their lives. She explores prayer, solitude, and worship, providing valuable insights and practical tools for nurturing a vibrant spiritual life. Throughout the book, Weaver shares personal anecdotes, biblical examples, and thought-provoking reflections that resonate with readers, inviting them to examine their hearts and priorities. She addresses familiar challenges and struggles individuals face seeking to balance their spiritual life with the demands of work, family, and other responsibilities. "Having a Mary Heart in a Martha World" inspires readers to seek a genuine and intimate relationship with God, allowing His presence to transform every aspect of their lives. It serves as a reminder that true fulfillment and purpose are found in the presence of God rather than in the pursuit of worldly achievements or external validation. Joanna Weaver's book offers a profound call to prioritize a heart posture of devotion, surrender, and genuine love for God amidst the distractions and pressures of the modern world. It is a guidebook for those yearning to deepen their spiritual journey and find rest.

Rest from Thinking

Another way of finding rest is taking a break from our thoughts. Our minds are often filled with constant ideas, worries, and anxieties that can overwhelm and drain us. The exact number of views a person has in one minute can vary widely depending on individual differences, circumstances, and mental state. It is challenging to quantify the precise number of thoughts as they can range from conscious reflections to fleeting and subconscious cognitive processes. Research suggests that the average person has thousands of views daily, amounting to many thoughts within a minute. It is important to note that not all opinions carry the same weight or impact on the mind. Some ideas may be fleeting and insignificant, while others may be more significant, meaningful, or impactful. Thoughts shape our perception of reality, influence our emotions, and drive our behaviors and actions. Positive reviews can uplift our mood, foster a sense of well-being, and enhance mental resilience. Conversely, negative or intrusive thoughts can lead to stress, anxiety, and negative emotional states. The quality and content of our thoughts can also influence our cognitive processes, decision-making, and problem-solving abilities. Positive and constructive reviews can promote clarity of thinking and facilitate creativity and innovation. Conversely, repetitive negative thoughts or cognitive distortions can impede rational thinking and hinder problem-solving skills. Awareness of our thoughts can help us understand their impact on our mental well-being. Practicing mindfulness allows us to observe our thoughts without judgment, choose which ideas to engage with or let go of, and cultivate a more balanced and positive thought pattern. Managing our thoughts and maintaining a healthy mental state requires attention, self-reflection, and sometimes seeking professional support when needed. With intentional practice and gentle guidance, we can discover moments of respite and calm within the chaos of our thoughts. This practice helps us detach from our reviews and find rest in the present moment. Another powerful tool for finding rest in our studies is letting go and surrendering. Often, we become attached to our thoughts, holding onto them tightly and allowing them to consume our mental and emotional energy. By consciously releasing our grip on these thoughts and surrendering them to a higher power or greater wisdom, we can experience a sense of relief and freedom. Offering our views allows us to trust in God and find rest, knowing that we are not alone in navigating life's challenges. Engaging in activities that bring us joy and help us shift our focus away from our thoughts can also offer a respite. Whether immersing ourselves in nature, pursuing creative endeavors, engaging in physical exercise, or spending time with loved ones, these activities temporarily distract us from our thoughts. Finding rest from our beliefs is not about suppressing or eradicating them completely but rather about creating a healthy relationship with them. It is about finding a balance between engaging with our thoughts when necessary and allowing ourselves moments of quiet and stillness.

"The Battlefield of the Mind" by Joyce Meyer is a book that explores the power of our thoughts and their impact on our emotions, behavior, and overall well-being. Meyer delves into the spiritual battle within our minds and offers practical insights and strategies for victory over negative thought patterns and destructive mindsets. Meyer emphasizes the importance of renewing our minds and aligning our thoughts with God's truth throughout the book. She addresses common struggles such as worry, fear, doubt, and condemnation and provides biblical principles and practical tools for overcoming these obstacles. Meyer's teachings draw heavily from Scripture, weaving together biblical wisdom and personal anecdotes to illustrate the power of our thoughts and the transformative potential of aligning our minds with God's Word. She emphasizes the role of faith, trust, and the renewing work of the Holy Spirit in transforming our thought patterns and renewing our minds. "The Battlefield of the Mind" equips readers with practical strategies for combating negative thoughts, such as replacing negative self-talk with positive affirmations, meditating on Scripture, and cultivating gratitude and praise. Meyer also addresses the importance of guarding our minds against external influences, such as media, toxic relationships, and worldly distractions that can negatively impact our thought lives. The book offers hope and encouragement to those struggling with negative thinking, reminding them to take control of their thoughts and align them with God's truth. Meyer's teachings guide readers to greater emotional and spiritual freedom, where they can experience the abundant life God desires for them. "The Battlefield of the

Mind" is an empowering resource for anyone seeking to overcome destructive thought patterns, find freedom from negative emotions, and experience a renewed mind. It serves as a reminder that victory begins in the mind and that by aligning our thoughts with God's truth, we can break free from the strongholds that hinder our growth and live a life of purpose, peace, and joy.

Rest from Fear of Judgement

Finding rest from the fear and burden of being judged by others can be a liberating and transformative experience. It involves embracing our identity in Christ and finding solace in His unconditional acceptance. One key aspect of finding rest from being judged as a Christian is understanding that our worth and value come from God alone. We are reminded in Scripture that we are fearfully and wonderfully made, deeply loved and fully accepted by our Heavenly Father. Embracing this truth allows us to find rest in knowing that our value is not determined by the opinions or judgments of others but by our relationship with God. It is also essential to cultivate a deep sense of self-acceptance and self-compassion. Recognizing that we are imperfect beings, saved by grace, enables us to extend the same dignity and compassion to ourselves. When we internalize God's forgiveness and embrace our imperfections, the judgments of others lose their power to define or diminish us. When our primary aim is to live according to God's Word and to honor Him in all that we do, the opinions of others become secondary. We find rest in knowing that our worth is rooted in obedience to God's commands and seeking His approval more than anything else. Additionally, immersing yourself in a supportive community of fellow believers is essential. You need to be with like-minded individuals who can provide encouragement and accountability. It helps us understand and can help us navigate the challenges of being judged. In such a community, we can find strength to rise above the judgments of others and remain steadfast in our faith. Practicing forgiveness is another vital aspect of finding rest from being judged. Forgiving those who believe or criticize us allows us to release bitterness or resentment and frees us from carrying the weight of their opinions. By entrusting judgment to God and extending forgiveness, we can find peace and rest, knowing that justice rests in His hands. Finally, finding rest from being judged as a Christian involves anchoring yourself in God's truth, nurturing self-acceptance, seeking His approval primarily, cultivating a supportive community, and practicing forgiveness. As we align our hearts with God's perspective and find our worth and identity in Him, we can experience a profound sense of rest, freedom, and peace that surpasses any judgment of others.

Come and Find Rest in Christ

Resting in Christ, who is One with God, goes beyond physical relaxation; it is a spiritual posture of surrender and trust. It is an invitation to lay down our worries, fears, and striving and to find comfort and security in the arms of our Savior. It is an invitation to release the world's weight and embrace the unshakable peace that can only be found in Him. His forgiveness washes over us, cleansing our souls and setting us free from the importance of our past mistakes. We can find rest from striving for acceptance and worth, knowing that our Creator deeply loves and values us. Finding rest in Christ is an ongoing journey—a daily choice to abide in His presence, seek

His wisdom, and align our hearts with His purposes. In this place of rest, we discover the true meaning of life, where we can experience joy, contentment, and a deep sense of belonging. Amid life's storms and challenges, Christ offers a refuge—a shelter from the chaos and a source of strength. He walks beside us, guiding us through the valleys and lifting us to the mountaintops. He invites us to cast our anxieties upon Him and trust that He will provide and sustain us. So, let us heed the invitation to come and find rest in Christ. Let us release our burdens, quiet our hearts, and enter His rest. We will experience a profound peace that surpasses all understanding as we abide in Him. May we find solace in His presence, draw strength from His love, and embark on a journey of restful surrender, knowing that in Christ, we find true and lasting rest for our souls.

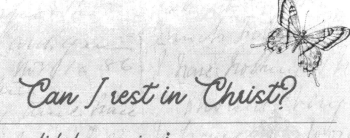

Can I rest in Christ?

if you did, keep going;

if you didn't, keep going;

Keep Going

EPILOGUE

I would love to listen to your journey of discovering rest in Christ. Your experiences and insights are valuable to me. Please email me if you have any questions or need guidance on where to start. I am here to provide support and understanding as we explore this path together. But I assure you that as you wholeheartedly seek Him, you will undoubtedly find rest in Christ, just as Jeremiah 33:3 promises, "Call to me, and I will answer you and tell you great and unsearchable things you do not know."

Lastly, I want to encourage you to explore the book "Gentle and Lowly" by Dane Ortlund. Within its pages, you will encounter a profound depiction of Christ's gentle and humble nature. This book beautifully reveals the heart of our Savior, who lovingly embraces us in our weariness and offers us true rest. As you delve into its contents, may you find solace and inspiration in the gentle presence of Christ, guiding you toward a deeper understanding of His restorative grace.

It is a beautiful journey filled with moments of self-discovery, spiritual growth, and deepening your relationship with the Lord. I am here to encourage and support you every step of the way, providing guidance and answering any questions you may have along this path of seeking and finding rest in Christ. Feel free to contact me via email at guirgisc@yahoo.com, and together we can embark on this transformative faith journey.

Selah

Reflect on Psalm 46

Psalm 46 is a powerful and inspiring passage that invites us to find refuge and strength in God, even amid the chaos, uncertainty, and upheaval. It is a reminder of God's persistent presence and power, who stands as our fortress and source of comfort. As I reflect on Psalm 46, I am struck by the recurring theme of God's unchanging nature and His ability to provide solace in times of trouble. The psalmist beautifully depicts a world shaken by natural disasters, upheavals, and conflicts, yet God remains steadfast and sovereign. This reminder gives me hope and reassurance that, regardless of the circumstances surrounding me, I can find refuge in the unchanging nature of God.

The psalmist speaks of God as a "very present help in trouble," reminding me that God is not a distant or disinterested deity but a loving and compassionate Father intimately involved in every aspect of our lives. He is ever-present, ready to extend His grace, strength, and comfort when we need it the most. This assurance fills me with a deep sense of peace, knowing I am never alone in my struggles and challenges. Verse 10 of the psalm resonates profoundly: "Be still and know that I am God." This verse is a gentle reminder to pause, be still, and cultivate a deep awareness of God's presence in a world that often demands constant activity and busyness. In those moments of stillness and surrender, we can truly encounter God and experience His peace that surpasses all understanding.

Moreover, the image of God as our refuge and fortress provides a sense of security and protection. It reminds me that no matter how tumultuous or uncertain the world may seem, I can find safety in God's presence. He is our ever-present shelter, a source of strength and courage in adversity. Psalm 46 points to the sovereignty of God and the assurance that He is in control, even when everything around us seems to be falling apart. It invites us to trust Him wholeheartedly and rest in His unwavering love and faithfulness. As I meditate on Psalm 46, I am encouraged to anchor my faith in God's unchanging nature, find solace in His presence, and confidently face life's challenges, knowing He is with me.

ABOUT THE AUTHOR

CAROLINE HANNA GUIRGIS is an inspiring author, motivational speaker, and advocate for positive change. With a profound belief that "The Beginning Starts at the End," Caroline embarked on a transformative journey that began with the publication of their debut book in 2017. Beyond the realm of writing, Caroline has dedicated herself to empowering individuals through captivating speeches and engaging presentations. As a motivational speaker, she has touched the lives of countless audiences, igniting the spark of hope and resilience within each listener. She also serves as a talk show host for the Christian Youth Channel. Through this platform, she engages with young individuals, providing guidance, encouragement, and a positive outlook rooted in their faith. Caroline's commitment to making a difference extends to her active involvement in non-profit work. She is deeply passionate about her role as a driving force behind The John Hanna Foundation, an organization currently spearheading the construction of a school for orphans in Uganda. The foundation strives to empower future generations and create a brighter tomorrow by providing education access.

Caroline's true passion lies in connecting with people, irrespective of their backgrounds or ambitions, to thrive together. She believes that by fostering meaningful connections, embracing diversity, and sharing experiences, individuals can transcend boundaries and collectively embark on a journey of growth and fulfillment. She embodies the spirit of compassion, inspiration, and empowerment through her writing, speaking engagements, philanthropic work, and personal relationships. Caroline invites you to join her on this unique path, where each encounter has the potential to transform lives and inspire greatness. Discover the transformative power of Caroline's words and let them guide you on a remarkable journey toward self-discovery, resilience, and living a peaceful and restful life.

Outside of her professional endeavors, Caroline finds joy and fulfillment in the roles of wife, mother, daughter, sister, aunt, cousin, and friend. These personal relationships exemplify the essence of love, support, and unwavering dedication.

Printed in the United States
by Baker & Taylor Publisher Services